AF440121

IN THE COMPANY OF THE QURAN

IN THE COMPANY OF THE QURAN

AN EXPLANATION OF SURAH YASIN

BY **FURHAN ZUBAIRI**

Printed in the United States of America

First Publishing, 2022

ISBN: 9798367256697

Cover design, layout, and typesetting: Mohammad Bibi
Typeset in Lato, Nassim, and KFGQPC Uthmanic Script HAFS
Arabic Symbols: KFGQPC Arabic Symbols 01

Contents

INTRODUCTION
XV

INTRODUCTION TO SŪRAH YĀSĪN
1

EXPLANATION OF SŪRAH YĀSĪN
7

Revelation From Allah ﷻ

The Story of the People of the Town

Signs in the Creation, Warning the Disbelievers & the Day of Resurrection

45

Arabic Letter	Transliteration	Sound
ء	ʾ	A slight catch in the breath, cutting slightly short the preceding syllable.
ا	ā	An elongated *a* as in *cat*.
ب	b	As in *best*.
ت	t	As in *ten*.
ث	th	As in *thin*.
ج	j	As in *jewel*.
ح	ḥ	Tensely breathed *h* sound made by dropping tongue into back of throat, forcing the air out.
خ	kh	Pronounced like the *ch* in Scottish *loch*, made by touching back of tongue to roof of mouth and forcing air out.
د	d	As in *depth*.
ذ	dh	A thicker *th* sound as in *the*.
ر	r	A rolled *r*, similar to Spanish.
ز	z	As in *zest*.
س	s	As in *seen*.
ش	sh	As in *sheer*.
ص	ṣ	A heavy *s* pronounced far back in the mouth with the mouth hollowed to produce full sound.
ض	ḍ	A heavy *d/dh* pronounced far back in the mouth with the mouth hollowed to produce a full sound.
ط	ṭ	A heavy *t* pronounced far back in the mouth with the mouth hollowed to produce a full sound.
ظ	ẓ	A heavy *dh* pronounced far back in the mouth with the mouth hollowed to produce a full sound.
ع	ʿ	A guttural sound pronouned narrowing the throat.
غ	gh	Pronounced like a throaty French *r* with the mouth hallowed.
ف	f	As in *feel*.
ق	q	A guttural *q* sound made from the back of the throat with the mouth hallowed.
ك	k	As in *kit*.
ل	l	As in *lip*.
م	m	As in *melt*.
ن	n	As in *nest*.
ه	h	As in *hen*.

	w (at the beg. of syllable)	As in *west*.
و	*ū* (in the middle of syllable)	An elongated *oo* sound, as in *boo*.
	y (at beg. of syllable)	As in *yes*.
ي	*ī* (in the middle of syllable)	An elongated *ee* sound, as in *seen*.

Used following the mention of Allah, God, translated as, "Glorified and Exalted be He."

Used following the mention of the Prophet Muḥammad, translated as, "May God honor and protect him."

Used following the mention of any other prophet or Gabriel, translated as, "May God's protection be upon him."

Used following the mention of the Prophet Muḥammad's Companions, translated as, "May God be pleased with them."

Used following the mention of a male Companion of the Prophet Muḥammad, translated as, "May God be pleased with him."

Used following the mention of a female Companion of the Prophet Muḥammad, translated as, "May God be pleased with her."

Used following the mention of two Companions of the Prophet Muḥammad, translated as, "May God be pleased with them both."

Used following the mention of the major scholars of Islam, translated as, "May God have mercy on them."

Used following the mention of a major scholar of Islam, translated as, "May God have mercy on him."

INTRODUCTION

Alḥamdulillāh, it truly is a great favor of Allah 🕮 that He's blessed us with both the ability and opportunity to study the Quran; His divine, uncreated, and eternal speech. The Quran is the last and final message sent for the guidance of humanity until the end of times. It is the greatest miracle given to the Prophet 🕮; a miracle that we can still see and experience till today. It is a book regarding which Allah 🕮 says, "[This is] a blessed Book which We have revealed to you, [O Muḥammad], that they might reflect upon its verses and that those of understanding would be reminded."[1] In this verse, Allah 🕮 describes the Quran with one single word, blessed. The Quran is blessed in every single way; everything about it is blessed, is full of blessings, and a source of blessings. Part of the blessing of the Quran is that those who learn it and teach it are the best of people. The Prophet 🕮 said, "The best among you are those who learn the Quran and teach it."[2] I ask Allah 🕮 through this small effort of mine to include me among the best of people.

I truly enjoy writing and compiling these works because I benefit from them in so many different ways. It allows me to look at my notes from when I was a student at Dār al-ʿUlūm Karachi, research, and read different tafāsīr that I otherwise wouldn't have time to do. I ask Allah 🕮 to accept this effort and place it on my scale of good deeds on the Day of Judgment.

Before beginning our exploration of Sūrah YāSīn, I would like to mention a few beneficial points that will help us approach the Quran as students,

---

1   كِتَابٌ أَنزَلْنَاهُ إِلَيْكَ مُبَارَكٌ لِّيَدَّبَّرُوا آيَاتِهِ وَلِيَتَذَكَّرَ أُولُو الْأَلْبَابِ - 38:29

2   Bukhārī, *k. faḍā'il al-Quran, b. khayrukum man taʿallama al-quran wa ʿallamahu,* 5027

particularly as seekers of guidance. It is always important to remember that the Quran, first and foremost, is a book of guidance. It's the last and final revelation of Allah ﷻ sent for the guidance of humanity, our guidance, until the end of times. Understanding the Quran as our own personal book of guidance makes it more relevant and real for us. Allah ﷻ says, "A guidance for mankind."[3] The Quran contains guidance for every single human being; young and old, male and female, believer, non-believer, Jew, Christian, Buddhist, Hindu, atheist, or agnostic. Anyone who approaches the Quran with an open heart and mind will receive some type of guidance. However, those who benefit most from the guidance found in the Quran are the people of God-consciousness. That is why Allah ﷻ also describes the Quran as "guidance for the God-conscious."[4] Everything that is mentioned in the Quran is mentioned as guidance for us. When reading the Quran we should focus on the practical and spiritual points of guidance that we can extract and understand.

Whenever Allah ﷻ mentions revelation, meaning the Quran being revealed, He uses four specific divine attributes:

1. al-ʿAzīz (the Almighty)
2. al-Ḥakīm (the All-Wise)
3. al-ʿAlīm (the All-Knowing), and
4. al-Raḥīm (the Very Merciful).

al-ʿAzīz is usually translated as the Almighty or the All-Powerful. It describes the One Who overpowers and can't be overpowered. It conveys the meanings of power, strength, victory, honor, dignity, and highness. When we're reading the Quran, we should always keep in mind that these are the words of al-ʿAzīz. The source of these words is power, honor, strength, and dignity. Through these words, we can acquire power, strength, victory, honor, dignity, and highness. As the Prophet ﷺ said, "Indeed Allah ﷻ raises some people with this book, and with it lowers others."[5]

The second attribute used is al-Ḥakīm, the All-Wise or the Most Wise.

---

3 هُدًى لِّلنَّاسِ - 2:185

4 هُدًى لِّلْمُتَّقِينَ - 2:2

5 Muslim, k. ṣalāh al-musāfirīn wa qaṣrihā, b. faḍl man yaqūmu bī al-qurān wa yuʿallim-uhu..., 817

The Quran is revelation from al-Ḥakīm, the absolutely and infinitely Most Wise. There is some deep divine wisdom behind each and every single chapter, verse, and word of the Quran. Every single verse, ruling, command, prohibition, and story has some divine wisdom that we as human beings can understand and sometimes can't. When Allah ﷻ instructs us to pray, fast, perform ḥajj, give zakāh, lower our gaze, and stay away from interest, He's done so out of His infinite wisdom.

The third attribute used with revelation is al-ʿAlīm, the All-Knowing. The One Whose knowledge is infinite, limitless, and never ending. The One Who knows every single thing; past, present, future, hidden and apparent, big and small. The One Whose knowledge encompasses every single thing. He ﷻ knows what's most beneficial for us as His creation. He knows best what will benefit us in this life and the next and He knows best what will harm us in this life and the next. Whatever He commands us to do, He does so because He knows that's what's best for us. Whatever He prohibits us from doing, He does so because He knows that's what's best for us. Throughout history, philosophers, thinkers, reformers, writers, and scientists have made mistakes and will continue to make mistakes. Allah ﷻ is free from all mistakes.

The fourth attribute mentioned in the context of revelation is al-Raḥīm, the Most-Merciful. Allah ﷻ is the Most-Merciful the Very Merciful. Allah ﷻ says, "And My mercy encompasses every single thing."[6] The nature of Divine mercy is that it's vast, encompassing, limitless, endless, infinite, and reaches all things. There isn't any Muslim or non-Muslim, obedient or disobedient individual who is not being constantly showered with Allah's mercy. Allah's ﷻ mercy is extremely vast. When He ﷻ created mercy, He ﷻ divided it into one hundred parts. He ﷻ sent down one part of mercy to this world and has kept the rest for the hereafter. The Prophet ﷺ said, "Allah has divided mercy into one hundred parts; and He retained with Him ninety-nine parts, and sent down to earth one part. Through this one part creatures deal with one another with compassion, so much so that an animal lifts its hoof over its young lest it should hurt it."[7] This is an amazing ḥadīth that helps us understand the magnitude of Allah's mercy. Part of His mercy is that He ﷻ sent the Quran to us as a book of guidance. He ﷻ sent us the Quran because of

---

6   وَرَحْمَتِي وَسِعَتْ كُلَّ شَيْءٍ - 7:156

7   Bukhārī, *k. al-adab, b. jaʿala Allah al-raḥmah miʾah juz*, 6000

His love for us.

Knowing that Allah ﷻ is al-Raḥīm is supposed to create a sense of hope in our hearts. In Arabic, this sense of hope is known as al-rajā'. It literally means hope or expectation, which is the exact opposite of despair. ibn al-Qayyim ﷺ described it saying, "Hope is to look at the vastness of Allah's mercy." It is to have hope in the mercy, forgiveness, acceptance, and grace of Allah ﷻ. It is said that al-rajā' is the essence of servitude to Allah ﷻ.

When reading and studying the Quran it is important to keep these four divine attributes of Allah ﷻ in mind. These words that we're reciting, listening to, and studying are the words of al-ʿAzīz, al-Ḥakīm, al-ʿAlīm and al-Raḥīm.

INTRODUCTION
TO SŪRAH YĀSĪN

Sūrah YāSīn is the 36th chapter of the Quran and is made up of 83 verses. It is characterized by short verses and a fast rhythm making it easy to recite and memorize. It is a Makkan sūrah; meaning it was revealed before the migration of the Prophet ﷺ from Makkah to Madinah. Some commentators mention that it's the 41st sūrah to be revealed; it was revealed after Sūrah al-Jinn and before Sūrah al-Furqān.

Similar to other Makkan revelation, YāSīn also discusses the three most fundamental aspects of our faith in its own unique and eloquent way. It discusses tawḥīd (oneness of Allah ﷻ) and the absolute power of Allah ﷻ, risālah (prophethood and messengership), and qiyāmah (resurrection and life after death). Out of these three fundamental themes, the most emphasis is given to the concept of resurrection.

Syed Quṭb ؒ writes, "This Makkan sūrah is characterized by short verses and a fast rhythm. Composed of 83 verses, it is slightly shorter in overall length than the preceding sūrah that contained only 45 verses. Such short verses together with the fast rhythm give the sūrah a special outlook. Its rhythm sounds successive beats, the effect of which is increased by the numerous images it draws, all leaving a profound impression. It shares the same main themes of all Makkan sūrahs, aiming to lay the foundation of faith. At the very outset, it dwells on the nature of revelation and the truth of the message."[8]

VIRTUES AND BENEFITS

Anas ﷺ narrates that the Prophet ﷺ said, "Indeed everything has a heart and the heart of the Quran is YāSīn. Allah ﷺ will record the recitation of ten Qurans for whoever reads YāSīn." [9]

From this ḥadīth, we learn about two distinct virtues:

1. It has been called the heart of the Quran, and
2. Reciting it carries a lot of reward.

It has been called the heart of the Quran because of its eloquence, beauty, clarity, and emotiveness. The heart is the most important organ of the body. Similarly, the spiritual heart is the most important part of our soul. The spiritual heart is the center of faith, understanding, recognition, God-consciousness, and spirituality. Sūrah YāSīn explains the fundamental beliefs of Islam in a very eloquent, beautiful, and effective style allowing its message and meanings to penetrate the heart. Soundness of faith rests on acknowledging resurrection and judgment and this sūrah details life after death in the most emphatic and effective way. It also contains overwhelming proofs, decisive signs, subtle meanings, eloquent admonition, and stern warnings that stir one's heart.

In another narration, it is reported that the Prophet ﷺ said, "Recite YāSīn upon your dead."[10] What is meant by "dead" in this ḥadīth is one who is about to leave this world. The Prophet ﷺ also said, "There is no dying person upon whom YāSīn is read except that Allah makes it [death] easy upon him."[11] One of the wisdoms of reciting YāSīn in the presence of someone who is about to leave this world is that it will remind them of Allah ﷺ and the Last Day. It will serve as a catalyst for them to turn their attention towards Allah ﷺ, repent, seek His forgiveness, and hope in His infinite mercy, grace, pardon, and forgiveness. This will lead towards the process of death becoming easy upon a person. It will also become a means for someone to leave this world with the kalimah (declaration of faith) on their tongue. The Prophet ﷺ said, "Whoever's last words are 'there is no deity worthy of worship except

---

9   Tirmidhī, *k. thawāb al-quran ʿan rasūlillāh, b. mā jāʾa fī faḍl YāSīn,* 2887

10   Abū Dāwūd, *k. al-janāʾiz, b. al-qirāʾah ʿind al-mayyit,* 3121

11   Qurṭubī, *al-Jāmiʿ li Aḥkām al-Quran,* 17:403

Allah' will enter Paradise."[12]

ibn ʿAbbās ﷺ said, "Whoever recites YāSīn in the morning will be given ease for that day until night. Whoever recites it at the beginning of the night will be given ease for the night until morning."[13] In another narration, it has been mentioned that whoever recites YāSīn at night will remain happy until the morning, and whoever recites it in the morning will remain happy until the night. The narrator of this report then said that someone who experienced this happiness narrated it to me.[14] This is one of the reasons why reciting YāSīn every morning is encouraged by scholars throughout the world. They describe a feeling of ease, happiness, and comfort as a result of this regular practice.

There are numerous narrations that detail the virtues, rewards, blessings, and benefits of reciting Sūrah YāSīn. Although many of these narrations may be classified as weak, and some perhaps may be extremely weak,[15] it is permissible to act upon them in hopes of receiving some of these blessings, rewards, and virtues. This is a sūrah that all of us should try to memorize and understand.

SUMMARY

In terms of subject matter, the sūrah can be divided into 8 parts:

1. Verses 1-12: Allah ﷻ consoles the Prophet ﷺ in order to strengthen his resolve, reaffirm him in his mission, and to provide him support. Allah ﷻ is reminding the Prophet ﷺ to not pay attention to what people say about him and his message; rather, he should ignore the slander, lies, and mockery because he's upon the truth.

2. Verses 13-32: Allah ﷻ mentions the story of the people of the town as a lesson, reminder, and warning to the people of Quraysh. Allah ﷻ is warning the non-believers of Makkah that if they continue to reject, ridicule, mock, persecute, and plot against the Prophet ﷺ,

---

12   Abū Dāwūd, *k. al-janāʾiz, b. fī al-talqīn,* 3116

13   al-Dārimī, *Sunan,* 3419

14   Qurṭubī, *al-Jāmiʿ li Aḥkām al-Quran,* 17:405

15   And this includes some of the narrations quoted above.

then they too will also be destroyed. At the same time, it is a reminder for the Prophet ﷺ and his Companions ﵂ to remain firm, strong, steadfast, and patient in the face of opposition, adversity, and persecution.

3. Verses 33-44: Speak about the signs and proofs that exist in Allah's ﷻ creation that prove His existence, oneness, magnificence, might, omnipotence, and absolute power.

4. Verses 45-47: Discuss the negative reaction of the nonbelievers after receiving the message of Islam.

5. Verses 48-58: Speak about the hereafter, specifically what will happen to the nonbelievers as opposed to what will happen to the believers.

6. Verses 59-68: Allah ﷻ elaborates the punishment of disbelief on the Day of Judgment and in Hellfire.

7. Verses 69-76: Once again establish the existence of Allah ﷻ and His oneness along with explaining some of the responsibilities of the Prophet ﷺ as a Prophet and Messenger.

8. Verses 77-83: Allah ﷻ ends the sūrah with a powerful and eloquent reminder about life after death.

EXPLANATION OF SŪRAH YĀSĪN

يٰسٓ ①

¹ YāSīn

Allah ﷻ starts this beautiful sūrah with two simple letters that are recited separately. There are many different sayings or explanations regarding these two letters. For example, some commentators say that these two letters are one of the divine names of Allah ﷻ. Others say it is one of the names or titles given to Muḥammad ﷺ. ibn ʿAbbās, ibn Masʿūd ﷺ and others mention that it means "O human." Others have said that it means "O leader of mankind" or that it is the title of the sūrah itself.¹⁶ The most correct position is that these are from the separated letters (al-ḥurūf al-muqaṭṭaʿah). There are 29 different chapters in the Quran that start with

---

16   Qurṭubī, *al-Jāmiʿ li Aḥkām al-Quran,* 17:408

separated letters. Allah ﷻ alone knows the meanings of these letters and He mentions them to highlight the miraculous and inimitable nature of the Quran. They are considered to be a secret from among the secrets of Allah ﷻ; meaning, no one knows what they truly mean except for the Creator Himself. They are from among the Mutashābihāt, those words or verses of the Quran whose meanings are hidden, unknown to us as human beings, or ambiguous. The definite meanings of these words and verses are unknown to us, highlighting our limited knowledge in comparison to the infinite and limitless knowledge of Allah ﷻ.

However, we do find that some great Companions of the Prophet ﷺ, as well as their students, sometimes gave meanings to these separated letters. For example, it's said that they are acronyms and each letter represents one of the names of Allah ﷻ. At the beginning of Sūrah Maryam, ibn ʿAbbās ﷺ narrated that, "'Kāf' is for Kāf (All-Sufficient), 'hā' is for Hād (the Guide), 'yā' is from Ḥakīm (All-Wise), "ʿayn' is from ʿAlīm (All-Knowing), and 'ṣād' is from Ṣādiq (Truthful)." However, these narrations can't be used as proof or to assign definitive meanings. They offer possibilities, but no one truly knows what they mean.

Naturally, the question that comes to our minds is why would Allah ﷻ start a sūrah with words that no one understands? The Scholars of the Quran have offered the following possible reasons:

1. To grab the attention of the listeners. One of the responsibilities of the Prophet ﷺ was to recite revelation, the Quran, to his community. When he would start his recitation with a series of separated letters it would capture the attention and intrigue of his audience.

2. To remind us that no matter how much we know there's always something that we don't know. The unknown nature of the separated letters helps keep us grounded and creates a sense of intellectual humility. No matter how much we advance as human beings in terms of knowledge, now matter how much we explore, research, discover, and uncover, our knowledge is very limited. Human knowledge is nothing compared to the infinite and limitless knowledge of Allah ﷻ.

3. These letters are the letters of the Arabic Language, and the Quran was revealed at a time that was the peak of eloquence of the language

and it was considered their identity. The Arabs took a lot of pride in their expertise in the Arabic Language, particularly composing prose and poetry that was extremely eloquent and beautiful. The Quran was revealed, challenging them spiritually and intellectually. The Arabs never heard these letters being used in such a majestic and unique way.

4. To bring attention to the miraculous and inimitable nature of the Quran. Human beings can never match the power, eloquence, beauty, and style of the Quran. Some scholars mention that these two letters and the way they are pronounced and recited is another proof of the divine protection and preservation of the Quran. The original script of the Quran was written without dots and vowels. The dots and vowels were added later on as the written language evolved to facilitate recitation. In the orginal maṣāḥif (copies of the Quran), a "yā" was written without the dots underneath it. A "bā," "tā," "thā," and "yā" were identical. The "sīn" and "shīn" were also identical. The fact that all of the expert recitors of the Quran recited the opening verse as "YāSīn" is a demonstration of the divine protection and preservation of the Quran.

وَٱلْقُرْءَانِ ٱلْحَكِيمِ ۞ إِنَّكَ لَمِنَ ٱلْمُرْسَلِينَ ۞ عَلَىٰ صِرَٰطٍ مُّسْتَقِيمٍ ۞ تَنزِيلَ ٱلْعَزِيزِ ٱلرَّحِيمِ ۞

[2] By the wise Quran, [3] You are truly one of the messengers [4] upon a straight path. [5] [This is] a revelation from the Almighty, Most Merciful,

Allah ﷻ starts the second verse by swearing an oath by the Quran. Generally, someone swears by something or takes an oath to highlight the importance of what they are saying and to prove that it is true. Oaths are common throughout the Quran and are used to emphasize certain undeniable truths and realities. Generally, Allah ﷻ takes an oath by one of His own magnificent and amazing creations that prove His existence, oneness, and limitless power. Sometimes He takes an oath by something that He has declared to be sacred. These oaths are taken to emphasize and prove certain realities and truths that Allah ﷻ wants humanity to accept and realize. When Allah ﷻ takes an oath it should cause us to pause and reflect; the Lord of the worlds Whose speech is the Truth is taking an oath. In this verse, Allah ﷻ is taking an oath by the Quran, His own divine revealed speech, to prove and emphasize that Muḥammad ﷺ is definitely a prophet and messenger. The fact that Allah ﷻ Himself swears by the Quran to declare this reality highlights the rank, status, and honor of the Prophet ﷺ.

Allah ﷻ describes the Quran with the adjective "ḥakīm," which comes from the root letters ḥā - kāf - mīm. These root letters convey the meanings of wisdom, judgment, rule, and decision. The word "ḥakīm" as an adjective conveys two meanings: wisdom and perfection.

The Quran is full of deep divine wisdom; it contains wisdom that is beyond any human conception or understanding of wisdom. The wisdom of the Quran provides guidance for every single aspect of our lives. Every single chapter, verse, word, concept, idea, theme, story, lesson, reminder, rule, instruction, parable, command, and prohibition is from the infinite, limitless, and comprehensive wisdom of Allah ﷻ. These are the words of al-Ḥakīm, the Most-Wise. The Quran is similar to a wise sage or elder that we come to for guidance and direction in our daily lives.

Syed Quṭb mentions a very beautiful point. He writes that wisdom is a quality of rational beings, and here it's being used to describe the Quran. Allah ﷻ is attributing a quality of life to His revelation; suggesting that it has a soul of its own, giving it qualities similar to those of a living person. Whenever we open our hearts to the Quran, it reveals more of its wisdom to us. Syed Quṭb says, "Although this is allegorical, nonetheless it describes a fact, bringing it closer to our minds' eye. This Quran has a soul of its own, giving it qualities similar to those of a living person with whom you have mutual responses and feelings. This takes place when you pay full attention to it and listen to it with your heart and soul. Whenever you open your faculties up to it, the Quran reveals to you more of its secrets. When you have lived for a while in the company of the Quran, you will long for its distinctive features, just as you long for the features of a close friend.

The Quran is certainly wise. It addresses everyone according to their ability; touching heartstrings, speaking in a measured way, and using a wisdom that suits each person. Furthermore, the Quran is full of wisdom. It educates people wisely, according to a straight, logical, and psychological system that releases all human potential and directs people to what is good and beneficial. It establishes a code of living that allows every human activity within the limits of its wise system."[17]

Another meaning of "al-ḥakīm" is perfect. Allah ﷻ is describing the Quran as being perfect and harmonious in terms of its words and meanings. The Quran is composed, organized, and structured in the most perfect way possible and is absolutely free of any faults, discrepancies, and contradictions. There are no contradictions in it in terms of words or meanings. It is free from all kinds of excess and deficiencies and it is balanced and harmonious. The Quran is perfect because it is coming from the source of perfection, Allah ﷻ.

Immediately after taking an oath by the wise and perfect Quran, Allah ﷻ mentions the subject of the oath; the reason why Allah ﷻ is swearing by the Quran. "You are truly one of the messengers upon a straight path." Allah ﷻ is swearing by the wise and perfect Quran and telling the Prophet ﷺ that he is a messenger, without a doubt, upon the truth. The path that he is upon - the path of Islam - is the Straight Path that leads towards success in this world and salvation in the next. The Straight Path is referring to the dīn of Islam, the comprehensive holistic way of life that Allah ﷻ has chosen for humanity. The path of Islam is upright, straight, direct, clear, and unambiguous, leading directly towards Allah ﷻ. Through this oath and statement, Allah ﷻ is consoling and comforting the Prophet ﷺ and, at the same time, refuting the false and baseless accusations of the Quraysh.

That is why the commentators mention that this verse serves two very important purposes:

1.   It's a consolation for the Prophet ﷺ - through these words, Allah ﷻ

---

17   Quṭb, *fī Ẓilāl al-Quran*, 5:2958

is consoling, comforting, and reassuring the Prophet ﷺ, reminding him not to be concerned about the baseless accusations of the Quraysh.

2. It's an emphatic rejection of the false claims of Quraysh - What they're saying about the Prophet ﷺ has no basis at all. Syed Quṭb writes, "The way this verse is phrased imparts a feeling that sending messengers is a well-recognized fact, with many past cases. This is not what is being proved here. Instead, what is being emphasized is that Muḥammad ﷺ is one of these messengers. The oath is addressed to Muḥammad ﷺ himself, not to those who deny his message, so as to place the oath, the Messenger ﷺ and the message above argument or discussion. It is a fact being stated by God about His Messenger ﷺ."[18]

Allah ﷻ then mentions another description of the Quran, "[This is] a revelation from the Almighty, Most-Merciful." Not only is the Quran full of wisdom, gems, and treasures, but it's also a revelation from Allah ﷻ the Almighty the Most-Merciful. Al-ʿAzīz is translated as the Almighty; the One Who overpowers and cannot be overpowered. It is derived from the root letters ʿayn-zā-zā, which convey the meanings of might, power, strength, and honor. Allah ﷻ, al-ʿAzīz, is the One Who is exalted in might, who can overcome and is not overcome, who is unassailable, invincible, who humiliates those who transgress, and who is honored. Allah ﷻ is al-Raḥīm, the Most-Merciful, Whose mercy is infinite, limitless, never-ending, and all-encompassing. The reason why these two specific attributes have been mentioned here is because when we look towards the Quran, we find that what it contains in terms of guidance, instruction, advice, glad-tidings, and warnings, comes from the two divine attributes of might and mercy.

Allah ﷻ then tells the Prophet ﷺ one of the reasons why he has been sent as a prophet and messenger.

---

18   Quṭb, *fī Ẓilāl al-Quran*, 5:2958

لِتُنذِرَ قَوْمًا مَّآ أُنذِرَ ءَابَآؤُهُمْ فَهُمْ غَـٰفِلُونَ ٦

⁶ so that you may warn a people whose forefathers were not warned, and so are heedless.

In this verse, Allah ﷻ is telling the Prophet ﷺ that He has sent him with the Quran, the wise and perfect scripture from the Almighty, the Most-Merciful, so that he may warn a people - a community - whose forefathers were not warned. The people whose "forefathers were not warned" is referring to the Arabs of that time. Since the time of Ibrāhīm ﷺ no prophet, messenger, or scripture had been sent to the Arabs for several centuries. Because no warner or messenger had come to them for some time, they were unaware of the truth, of belief, guidance, morality, and divine law. They were in a state of ghaflah, which is translated as heedlessness. They were unaware of true belief and were drowning in the darkness of idol worship and immorality. Ghaflah is one of the worst afflictions of the heart. A heedless heart is unable to see, process, or understand the truth. The truth is right in front of their eyes, as clear as the sun, but they are unable to see it, let alone notice it or feel it.

The Prophet ﷺ is being reminded that one of his main responsibilities is to warn his community, to snap them out of their state of ghaflah. One of the primary objectives of revelation is to warn against disbelief, immorality, heedlessness, carelessness, and everlasting punishment. The Prophet ﷺ was sent as a giver of glad tidings and a warner. He was sent as "bashīr" and "nadhīr." Bashīr is one who gives glad tidings and good news. The Prophet ﷺ gave glad tidings and good news of blessings, mercy, grace, forgiveness, salvation, and Paradise to those who accepted the truth and believed. Nadhīr is one who warns with genuine care, concern, and sincerity. The Prophet ﷺ warned those who rejected the truth and disbelieved about punishment, both in this world and the next.

Allah ﷻ then tells us about those people who He knew would choose disbelief and die upon it.

لَقَدْ حَقَّ ٱلْقَوْلُ عَلَىٰٓ أَكْثَرِهِمْ فَهُمْ لَا يُؤْمِنُونَ ﴿٧﴾

⁷ The word has indeed come true about most of them, so they will not believe.

"The word" in this verse refers to the divine decree that "most of them" will not believe; that they will reject the truth and as a result be deserving of punishment in the Hereafter. "Most of them" is referring to the sworn and open enemies of the Prophet ﷺ from Quraysh that opposed him at every opportunity. Allah ﷻ had willed and decreed from pre-eternity that these individuals would not accept the truth, based on their own volition and choice. Allah ﷻ, through His infinite knowledge and wisdom, knew that these people, through their own free will, would choose disbelief and be persistent in it, denying the truth till their death. This does not mean that they were compelled, coerced, or forced to disbelieve; rather, it means that Allah ﷻ was aware of the fact that they would be stubborn and choose to disbelieve even after they had been warned. They chose not to believe and reject the Prophet's warning through their own individual will.

This verse also serves as a source of comfort and consolation for the Prophet ﷺ. Allah ﷻ is reminding the Prophet ﷺ that his responsibility is simply to convey the message of guidance. He is not responsible for people choosing to accept it or deny it.

Allah ﷻ then gives two examples or metaphors of the state of their disbelief. "At this point, the sūrah draws an image of their psychological condition, and we see them with chains around their necks, barriers separating them from divine guidance, and with a cover over their eyes depriving them of the ability to see."[19]

إِنَّا جَعَلْنَا فِي أَعْنَاقِهِمْ أَغْلَالًا فَهِيَ إِلَى ٱلْأَذْقَانِ فَهُم مُّقْمَحُونَ ۝ وَجَعَلْنَا مِنْ بَيْنِ أَيْدِيهِمْ سَدًّا وَمِنْ خَلْفِهِمْ سَدًّا فَأَغْشَيْنَٰهُمْ فَهُمْ لَا يُبْصِرُونَ ۝

⁸ We have placed iron collars on their necks, so they are reaching up to their chins, and their heads are forced to remain upwards. ⁹ And We have placed a barrier in front of them and a barrier behind them, and (thus) they are encircled by Us; so they do not see.

Allah ﷻ is providing a physical description that describes the spiritual bankruptcy of the non-believers of Quraysh. This figurative description helps us understand their inability to see the truth even though it is right in front of their eyes. Allah ﷻ is telling us that He has placed an iron collar on their necks; an iron collar similar to those that were placed around the necks of dangerous criminals in the past. Generally, there

---

19   Quṭb, fī Ẓilāl al-Quran, 5:2959

is a chain that binds and shackles the hands of the criminals to their necks as well. Allah ﷻ is illustrating the picture of a prisoner bound and shackled with a collar and chains. This iron collar reaches their chin, forcing their head and eyes upwards, so they are unable to see what's right in front of them. This is a figurative description of their spiritual reality. Despite the clarity of the truth that can be seen with open eyes, they have failed to see it, as if their heads and eyes are forced upwards by the collars around their necks. This figurative description can be understood as a metaphor for their pride and arrogance. It shows that one of the reasons for refusing to accept the truth and rejecting the Prophet's ﷺ warning was their own pride and arrogance; their pride and arrogance blinded them from accepting the truth.

In the second description, Allah ﷻ tells us that He has "placed a barrier in front of them and a barrier behind them, and (thus) they are encircled by Us." Allah ﷻ has placed some sort of barrier that surrounds them and restricts their sight, vision, and movement. This barrier cuts them off from their surroundings, causing them to be unaware of what is going on around them. This can be understood as a figurative expression for them having surrounded themselves with ignorance and stubbornness that prevents them from accepting the truth. All of the pathways of īmān entering into their hearts have been blocked and sealed off. al-Qurṭubī ﷺ mentions another very interesting explanation, saying that the "barrier in front of them" is them being fooled and deceived by the life of this world and the "barrier behind them" is their rejection of life after death. As a result of these two "barriers," their entire life is encircled by disbelief. [20]

Amazingly, we meet and interact with people that fit into both of these descriptions. There are individuals who are too proud to accept the truth even though they recognize it deep down in their hearts. Their ego and self-aggrandizement prevent them from submitting to the truth. This is exactly how the Prophet ﷺ defined arrogance. He ﷺ defined it as "rejecting the truth and belittling people."[21] There are others who have intentionally put blinders in front of their eyes; the truth is right in front of them but they are unable to see it. They have been spiritually blinded and barriers have been placed around them, preventing them from seeing, accepting, and submitting to the truth. For example, there are individuals who have dedicated their

---

20 Qurṭubī, *al-Jāmiʿ li Aḥkām al-Quran*, 17:418

21 Muslim, *k. al-īmān, b. taḥrīm al-kibr wa bayānuhu*, 91

lives to science and spend countless hours observing and researching some of the most amazing creations of Allah ﷻ, yet still do not believe in the Divine. The result of their inability to see or understand the truth is that the Prophet's warning has no effect on them.

وَسَوَآءٌ عَلَيْهِمْ ءَأَنذَرْتَهُمْ أَمْ لَمْ تُنذِرْهُمْ لَا يُؤْمِنُونَ ۝

[10] It is the same whether you warn them or not—they will never believe.

Through this verse, Allah ﷻ is consoling, comforting, and reassuring His beloved Messenger ﷺ. The Prophet ﷺ had genuine concern for the safety, protection, and salvation of his people. His mission was to save as many people as possible from eternal torment through the light of faith and guidance. When people would reject the truth, it would pain the Prophet ﷺ. The pain he felt was not personal; rather, it was a result of his knowledge regarding what that rejection leads to. Allah ﷻ is reminding the Prophet ﷺ that because the non-believers of Quraysh are spiritually deaf, dumb, and blind, "it is the same whether you warn them or not—they will never believe." They will never believe because of the barriers that are preventing īmān from entering their hearts. Your warning and reminding will not benefit them in any way as long as they are unwilling and unable to accept the truth. They have been so blinded by their beliefs and are so arrogant and proud, that no matter what you say or do, it will not affect them. Warning does not give life to a heart; rather, it only alerts a heart that is alive and ready to receive guidance.

Allah ﷻ then continues to console and reassure the Prophet ﷺ by reminding him that his warning only affects those who believe in the Quran and fear Him.

إِنَّمَا تُنذِرُ مَنِ ٱتَّبَعَ ٱلذِّكْرَ وَخَشِيَ ٱلرَّحْمَٰنَ بِٱلْغَيْبِ ۖ فَبَشِّرْهُ بِمَغْفِرَةٍ وَأَجْرٍ كَرِيمٍ ۝

¹¹ You can only warn those who follow the Reminder and are in awe of the Most Compassionate without seeing Him. So give them good news of forgiveness and an honorable reward.

Your warning benefits and affects individuals who possess two unique qualities and characteristics:

1. Those who follow the Reminder, and
2. Those who are in awe of the Most Compassionate without seeing Him.

The word "dhikr" is one of the names or titles of the Quran. It has been called "the Reminder" because it reminds the audience of the existence, oneness, might, power, and glory of Allah ﷻ. It also reminds humanity about fundamental concepts, responsibilities, values, principles, morals, and ethics. Whenever we recite the Quran or listen to it we are reminded about Allah ﷻ, our relationship with Him, His rights upon us, our rights upon each other, manners, etiquettes, character, virtues, worship, submission, servitude, the purpose of life, morality, right and wrong, the finite nature of this life, the eternal nature of the life to come, resurrection, life after death, accountability, judgment, reward and punishment, and paradise and hell. Following the Reminder refers to first and foremost accepting and acknowledging that it is the speech of Allah ﷻ, revealed to His last and final Messenger ﷺ, believing in it, reciting it, understanding it, reflecting upon its meanings, and implementing its guidance into our daily lives.

Following the Quran as described above nurtures and develops khashyah, positive fear, of Allah ﷻ. This is the second quality of those who truly benefit from the warning and guidance of the Prophet ﷺ. Khashyah is a particular type of fear that comes from reverence, awe, respect, and love. We fear Allah ﷻ because of our love, reverence, awe, and respect of Him. It is this fear that helps keep us firm and steadfast upon the Straight Path. The word choice of Allah ﷻ is significant and oftentimes conveys deeper meanings. Here, Allah ﷻ chooses to refer to Himself with the name ar-Raḥmān, the Most Compassionate. This reminds us that although we do fear the anger and displeasure of Allah ﷻ and His punishment, He is also the Most Compassionate. Allah ﷻ is the One Whose mercy is infinite and encompasses all things. Allah ﷻ forgives all sins, mistakes, shortcomings, and acts of disobedience as long as we turn back to Him through seeking forgiveness and repentance. Our relationship with Allah ﷻ is guided through both fear and hope. We fear His punishment, but at the same time, we have hope in His mercy, grace, forgiveness, and pardon.

Another unique aspect about this fear, is that they fear Allah ﷻ without having seen Him. Belief in the unseen, al-ghayb, is a fundamental aspect of our īmān. Although we have never seen Allah ﷻ, we still have absolute certainty in His existence, oneness, might, and power. We have absolute certainty that He alone created the universe and everything it contains, that He is absolutely unique, and that He alone is deserving and worthy of worship. Although we have never seen Allah ﷻ, there are manifest signs of His existence all around us. The entire world and everything in it is an open and clear book, teaching us about the Divine.

Allah ﷻ instructs the Prophet ﷺ to give good news and glad tidings of forgiveness and a generous reward to those who follow the Reminder and fear the Most Compassionate. A person who follows the guidance of the Quran to the best of their abilities and fears Allah ﷻ will be granted forgiveness for their sins, mistakes, shortcomings, faults, and acts of disobedience. In addition to that, they will be given a generous reward, which is referring to Paradise. Through this verse, Allah ﷻ is giving a us a very simple roadmap that leads towards forgiveness and salvation in the next life; living our lives according to the guidance of the Quran and fearing Allah ﷻ.

A major theme of the opening verses of Sūrah Yāsīn is prophethood, which is one of the most fundamental aspects of our faith. In the next verse, Allah ﷻ reminds us about another fundamental aspect of our faith; life after death. He ﷻ reminds us that we will all be brought back to life and held accountable for our deeds. We are reminded that everything we say or do is being recorded.

إِنَّا نَحْنُ نُحْيِ ٱلْمَوْتَىٰ وَنَكْتُبُ مَا قَدَّمُوا وَءَاثَـٰرَهُمْ وَكُلَّ شَىْءٍ أَحْصَيْنَـٰهُ فِىٓ إِمَامٍ مُّبِينٍ ﴿١٢﴾

¹² It is certainly We Who resurrect the dead, and write what they send forth and what they leave behind. Everything is listed by Us in a perfect Record.

In the first part of this verse, Allah ﷻ is establishing that life after death is an absolute truth and reality. He ﷻ is informing us that He alone is the One Who will bring the dead back to life on the Day of Judgment. In the second part of the verse, Allah ﷻ describes the concepts of accountability, reward, and punishment.

"It is certainly We Who resurrect the dead." Meaning, without a doubt, Allah ﷻ will bring us back to life on the Day of Judgment to hold us accountable for our deeds. Allah ﷻ is emphatically stating that He will bring the dead back to life. One of the reasons for this emphasis is to serve as a direct response to the non-believers of Quraysh who considered the idea of resurrection to be far-fetched.

Life after death is intrinsically linked to the concepts of reward and punishment, accountability, Paradise and Hell. That is one of the reasons why Allah ﷻ then highlights that He has "what they send forth and what they leave behind" recorded. Every single thing we say and do as human beings is recorded in our book of deeds. Allah ﷻ has appointed two Angels with every single human being, whose responsibility is to record everything they say and do, both the good and the bad. Allah ﷻ refers to our statements and deeds as what we send forward, because it is as if we are sending them forward for judgment and accountability. Our words and deeds - good and bad, righteous and shameful - will be for or against us on the Day of Judgment. As Allah ﷻ says in Sūrah al-Infiṭār regarding the Day of Judgment, "⸢Then⸣ each soul will know what it has sent forth or left behind."[22] Allah ﷻ also says, "O believers! Be mindful of Allah and let every soul look to what ⸢deeds⸣ it has sent forth for tomorrow. And fear Allah, ⸢for⸣ certainly Allah is All-Aware of what you do."[23]

There is a very beautiful ḥadīth qudsī in which Allah ﷻ provides a general principle for the scale that He ﷻ uses for reward and punishment. The ḥadīth highlights the infinite grace and mercy of Allah ﷻ along with His ultimate justice. ibn ʿAbbās ﷺ narrates from the Messenger of Allah ﷺ, who narrates from his Lord: "Verily Allah the Most High has written down the good deeds and the evil deeds, and then explained it [by saying]: 'Whosoever intended to perform a good deed, but did not do it, then Allah writes it down with Himself as a complete good deed. And if he intended to perform it and then did perform it, then Allah writes it down with Himself as from ten good deeds up to seven hundred times, up to many times multiplied. And if he intended to perform an evil deed, but did not do it, then Allah writes it down with Himself as a complete good deed. And if he intended it [i.e., the evil deed] and then performed it, then Allah writes it down as one evil deed.'"[24]

Just as our deeds, both good and bad, are being recorded so are the ef-

---

22   عَلِمَتْ نَفْسٌ مَّا قَدَّمَتْ وَأَخَّرَتْ - 82:5

23   يَا أَيُّهَا الَّذِينَ آمَنُوا اتَّقُوا اللَّه وَلْتَنظُرْ نَفْسٌ مَّا قَدَّمَتْ لِغَدٍ وَاتَّقُوا اللَّه إِنَّ اللَّه - 59:18 خَبِيرٌ بِمَا تَعْمَلُونَ

24   Bukhārī, k. al-riqāq, b. man hamma bī ḥasanah aw bī sayyi'ah, 6491

fects, consequences, traces, and impact of our deeds. Our actions and words have consequences, both positive and negative. These consequences can inspire people towards good or bad. The word āthār is the plural of athar, which is translated as trace, vestige, track, sign, or mark. According to several scholars of tafsīr, it refers to the outcome, impact, effect, and consequences of deeds and statements - good or bad - that show up later on and continue to have an influence. The good we leave behind will bring us reward and the bad we leave behind will bring us sin. The Prophet ﷺ said, "Whoever introduces a good practice that is followed after him, will have a reward for that and the equivalent of their reward, without that detracting from their reward in the slightest. Whoever introduces an evil practice that is followed after him, will bear the burden of sin for that and the equivalent of their burden of sin, without that detracting from their burden in the slightest."[25] The Prophet ﷺ also said, "When the son of Adam dies, all of his deeds come to an end except for three: knowledge that is beneficial, a righteous child who prays for him, and ongoing charity that he leaves behind."[26]

al-Qurṭubī ﷺ writes that the "traces" of a person that remain and are mentioned after they leave this world, both the good and the bad, will be recompensed. Examples of good "traces" are knowledge that they taught, books they authored, or a building they constructed, such as a masjid or bridge. Examples of evil traces are tools and instruments that were produced to take people away from the remembrance of Allah ﷺ. [27]

According to another interpretation, the word āthār is referring to the footsteps of those who walk towards the masjid for prayer. This interpretation is based on a ḥadīth that is cited as the background of revelation for this particular verse. Abū Saʿīd al-Khudrī ﷺ narrates that Banu Salimah's dwellings were on the outskirts of Madinah, so they wanted to relocate closer to the Masjid. Then this verse was revealed: 'It is certainly We Who resurrect the dead, and write what they send forth and what they leave behind. Everything is listed by Us in a perfect Record.' So the Messenger of Allah ﷺ said, "Your steps are recorded, so do not relocate."[28] In another version, Jābir ﷺ narrates that Banu Salimah decided to move near the mosque because there were

---

25 ibn Mājah, k. al-muqaddimah, b. man sanna sunnah ḥasanah aw sayyi'ah, 207

26 Muslim, k. al-waṣiyyah, b. mā yalḥaqu al-insān min al-thawāb baʿda wafātihi, 1631

27 Qurṭubī, al-Jāmiʿ lī Aḥkām al-Quran, 17:420

28 Tirmidhī, k. tafsīr al-quran ʿan rasūlillāh, b. wa min sūrah yāsīn, 3226

some vacant plots near it. When this news reached the Messenger of Allah ﷺ he said, "O Banu Salimah! [Remain in] Your homes because your footsteps are recorded." After hearing this, Banu Salimah said, "Moving closer would not have made us happy."[29]

There are several other narrations from the Prophet ﷺ that mention the virtues, rewards, and blessings for walking to the masjid. The Prophet ﷺ said, "The reward of prayer offered by a person in congregation is twenty five times greater than that of prayer offered in one's house or in the market (alone). And that is because if he performs ablution and does it with excellence and then proceeds to the mosque with the sole intention of praying, then for every step he takes towards the mosque, he is elevated one degree in reward and one sin is erased. When he completes his prayer, the Angels continue to send blessings upon him as long as he remains in his place of prayer. They say, 'O Allah! Bestow Your blessings upon him, be Merciful and kind to him.' And one is regarded in prayer as long as one is waiting for the prayer."[30]

"Everything is listed by Us in a perfect Record." Meaning, all of our statements and actions are recorded in our book of deeds, which will be given to us on the Day of Judgment. The "perfect Record" in this verse is referring to the book of deeds; the record or register in which all our deeds, good and bad, big and small, public and private are recorded. This book of deeds serves as a comprehensive witness and record of whatever we say or do in the life of this world. The righteous will receive it in their right hand and the wicked will receive it in their left hand. We ask Allah ﷻ to make us amongst those who receive it in their right!

That brings us to the end of the first passage of Sūrah YāSīn. So far, the Sūrah has discussed the truthfulness and beauty of the Quran, the Messenger of Allah ﷺ, and the concept of there being messengers sent by Allah ﷻ to deliver His message to humanity. The Sūrah has also told us that there are two distinct groups of human beings with respect to Allah's message and His messengers; those who accept the truth and those who reject it. Allah ﷻ describes the condition of those who consciously choose to reject the truth and those who choose to accept it. The first passage also reminds us of life after death and the concepts of accountability, reward, and punishment.

---

29 Muslim, *k. al-masājid wa mawāḍiʿ al-ṣalāh, b. faḍl kathrah al-khuṭā ilā al-masājid,* 665

30 Bukhārī, *k. al-adhān, b. faḍl ṣalāh al-jamāʿah,* 647

The next set of verses, 13-32, deals with the story of the people of a particular town. The story is given the title Qiṣṣah Aṣḥāb al-Qaryah, literally, the Story of the People of the Town. In this passage, Allah ﷻ is giving a veiled threat and warning to the people of Quraysh regarding their attitude and behavior towards the Prophet ﷺ and the community of believers. If they continue to reject and deny the truth, oppose the Prophet ﷺ and his message, and persecute his companions, then their fate will be similar to the people of this town. It also serves as a consolation to the Prophet ﷺ and his Companions, reminding them to remain patient, steadfast, strong, and firm. The story reassures the community of believers by reminding them that Allah's divine help, aid, and assistance is with them.

وَٱضْرِبْ لَهُم مَّثَلًا أَصْحَـٰبَ ٱلْقَرْيَةِ إِذْ جَآءَهَا ٱلْمُرْسَلُونَ ۝ إِذْ أَرْسَلْنَآ إِلَيْهِمُ ٱثْنَيْنِ فَكَذَّبُوهُمَا فَعَزَّزْنَا بِثَالِثٍ فَقَالُوٓا إِنَّآ إِلَيْكُم

مُّرْسَــلُونَ ١٤

¹³ Give them an example [O Prophet] of the residents of a town, when the messengers came to them. ¹⁴ We sent them two messengers, but they rejected both. So We reinforced [the two] with a third, and they declared, "We have indeed been sent to you [as messengers]."

Allah ﷻ is instructing His messenger ﷺ to tell the people of Makkah about the story of the people of a particular town. The Quran does not specifically mention which town this is, who these people are, where this town is, or even who the messengers are. Generally speaking, whenever there is a story mentioned in the Quran, it is not mentioned completely in chronological order from beginning to end with all its details. Rather, it is mentioned for a reason or purpose. One of those reasons is so that we can learn and extract lessons, morals, and reminders from it. The stories of the Quran are not entertainment or simple historical facts. Rather, they are there so that we can study them and derive lessons, morals, and reminders that we can use in our daily lives. That is one of the reasons why we find that Allah ﷻ has not related a complete story in chronological order, from beginning to end, with all its details. The only exception to this, and it is a partial exception, is the narrative of Prophet Yūsuf ﷺ mentioned in Sūrah Yūsuf. He ﷺ only relates those parts of the story that are relevant and related to guidance. As Allah ﷻ says, "Surely, in the narratives of these, there is a lesson for the people of understanding. It is not an invented story, rather, a confirmation of what has been before it, and an elaboration of everything, and guidance and mercy for a people who believe."³¹ For example, one of the objectives of this story is to serve as a warning to the people of Makkah and as reassurance for the Prophet ﷺ and his Companions. In Sūrah Hūd, Allah ﷻ tells us, "We narrate to you all such stories from the events of the messengers as We strengthen your heart therewith. And in these (stories) there has

---

31   12:111 - لَقَـدْ كَانَ فِى قَصَصِهِـمْ عِـبْرَةٌ لِّأُولِى الْأَلْبَابِ مَا كَانَ حَدِيثًا يُفْـتَرَىٰ وَلَـكِن تَصْدِيـقَ الَّذِى بَـيْنَ يَدَيْـهِ وَتَفْصِيـلَ كُلِّ شَىْءٍ وَهُـدًى وَرَحْمَـةً لِّقَـوْمٍ يُؤْمِنُـونَ

come to you the truth, a good counsel and a reminder to those who believe."[32]

This same method of relating stories is used in narrating this story; only the parts that are related to guidance have been mentioned. There is no mention of the remaining parts of the story that are purely historical or geographical. However, the commentators of the Quran, by studying historical and religious sources, have been able to provide these details. The majority of mufassirūn (scholars of tafsir) agree that this town was Anṭākiyah, the ancient town of Antioch, and that the Messengers that were sent to them were the disciples of ʿĪsā ﷺ.

Again, Allah ﷻ is telling the Prophet ﷺ to give the non-believers of Quraysh the example of this particular town as a veiled threat and warning. If you continue to disbelieve, reject the truth, and oppose the Prophet ﷺ and his Companions out of stubbornness, hatred, pride and arrogance, then you will also be destroyed. You will face the same fate as the people of Antioch who were destroyed for their refusal to accept the truth and their persecution of the righteous.

Allah ﷻ introduces the story saying, "When the messengers came to them." According to several Tafsīr authorities, the messengers here are referring to the disciples of ʿĪsā ﷺ.[33] "We sent them two messengers, but they rejected both. So We reinforced [the two] with a third, and they declared, 'We have indeed been sent to you [as messengers]'." Allah ﷻ instructed ʿĪsā ﷺ to send two of his disciples to Antioch in order to invite them towards the truth; towards belief in Allah ﷻ alone without any partners, his prophethood, and life after death. The two messengers of ʿĪsā ﷺ arrived in the town and immediately went to work. However, the people responded to them with rejection and opposition. They rejected both of them, and according to some narratives, had them beaten and imprisoned. "So We reinforced [the two] with a third." Allah ﷻ instructed ʿĪsā ﷺ to send a third messenger as support and reinforcement for the first two and they declared, "We have indeed been sent to you [as messengers]."

It is very interesting to see how history repeats itself. Throughout history, the initial response of every community towards its messenger has been

---

32 وَكُلًّا نَّقُصُّ عَلَيْكَ مِنْ أَنبَاءِ الرُّسُلِ مَا نُثَبِّتُ بِهِ فُؤَادَكَ وَجَاءَكَ فِي هَـٰذِهِ الْحَقُّ - 11:120 وَمَوْعِظَةٌ وَذِكْرَىٰ لِلْمُؤْمِنِينَ

33 Other mufassirūn are of the opinion that these were three messengers of Allah ﷻ that were sent to the town of Antioch to invite them towards belief in Allah ﷻ alone without any partners.

skepticism, opposition, and rejection. This is exactly how the leadership of Quraysh initially responded to the message and mission of the Prophet ﷺ.

al-Qurṭubī ﷻ mentions the story of the three disciples in his famous work of tafsīr. The details of the story are from different sources[34], some of which may be true and some of which may be untrue. The narrative helps fill in some of the historical details of the story and can be useful in extracting certain lessons and morals. It is important to note that these details should not be taken as definitive; what we know for sure about the story is what Allah ﷻ has mentioned explicitly in the Sūrah. The following is what al-Qurṭubī ﷻ relates[35]:

'Īsā ﷺ sent two messengers to the people of Antioch. On the outskirts of the town, they met an old man grazing a few sheep of his by the name of Ḥabīb al-Najjār. They invited him towards belief in Allah ﷻ saying, "We are messengers of 'Īsā ﷺ." Ḥabīb requested them to show him sort of a miracle. They replied saying that they were given the ability, through the permission of Allah ﷻ, to cure the ill. It just so happened that Ḥabīb had a child who was ill and bed-ridden. The messengers passed their hands over the child, and by the permission of Allah ﷻ, he was cured. As a result of witnessing this miracle, Ḥabīb accepted the truth and and became a believer. Eventually, news of these two messengers who can miraculously cure the ill spread through the town and they were able to cure a large number of people.

The town was ruled by a king who worshipped idols. He found out about these two messengers and sent for them in order to ask about them and their message. They said that they were the messengers of 'Īsā ﷺ. He then asked why they had come to his town. They responded saying that they had come to cure the blind, the leper, and the ill with the permission of Allah ﷻ, and to call people towards the worship of Allah ﷻ alone. The king immediately had them imprisoned and lashed a hundred times.

News of their imprisonment and torture reached 'Īsā ﷺ and he sent a third messenger to support them and their cause. He came and lived among the people in a clandestine manner until he was able to win favor with them and they became comfortable with him. The king was informed about him and he was able to win some favor with the king as well. Outwardly, he dis-

---

34   It is most likely that these details come from Judeo-Christian sources known in Tafsīr literature as Isrāīliyāt.

35   This is not an exact translation. I used literary license for the sake of readability.

played that he was upon the religion of the king and, eventually, he gained an audience with the king. One day he asked the king about the two messengers he had imprisoned. He said, "I heard you have imprisoned two people for calling you towards belief in Allah 🕮 alone. Why don't you summon them and ask them their story?" The king replied that his anger prevented him from doing so.

Again he suggested summoning them and the king did so. This third messenger, who was undercover, asked them, "What is your proof for your claim of being messengers?" They said, "We can cure the blind and the leper." A young boy was brought to them who was born without eyes in his eye sockets. The two messengers supplicated to Allah 🕮 and miraculously he was given eyes and the ability to see.

The king was shocked and amazed. He said that there is a young boy who passed away seven days ago and I have not buried him because I'm waiting for his father to return. Can your Lord bring him back to life? The two messengers supplicated to Allah 🕮 openly and the third messenger supplicated silently, and the boy came back to life and said, "I passed away seven days ago as a polytheist. As a result, I was made to enter seven valleys of Hell. I'm warning you about the religion you are upon. Believe in Allah 🕮 alone without any partners. The gates of Heaven were then opened for me and I saw a young man with a beautiful face interceding on behalf of these three messengers. Allah 🕮 then brought me back to life and I bear witness that there is no one worthy of worship except Allah alone without partner, that 'Īsā 🕮 is the spirit of Allah and His word, and that they are the messengers of Allah." The people responded in surprise saying, "Is this person with the king also a messenger?" He said, "Yes, and he is the best of them." He then announced that he is one of the messengers of 'Īsā 🕮 sent to them. His words had an impact on the king's heart and so he invited him towards belief. The king along with a large number of people, then accepted the truth while others continued to disbelieve.[36]

In the Quran, Allah 🕮 simply tells us that He 🕮 sent two messengers to the people of this particular town. The messengers invited them towards worshiping Allah 🕮 alone without any partners, and they responded with rejection and opposition. Allah 🕮 then supported them by sending a third messenger, establishing definitive proof and evidence upon the people of

---

36   Qurṭubī, *al-Jāmiʿ li Aḥkām al-Quran*, 17:425

this town. Allah ﷻ then tells us some of the conversations that took place between the messengers and the people of the town.

قَالُوا مَآ أَنتُمْ إِلَّا بَشَرٌ مِّثْلُنَا وَمَآ أَنزَلَ ٱلرَّحْمَـٰنُ مِن شَىْءٍ إِنْ أَنتُمْ إِلَّا تَكْذِبُونَ ۝

¹⁵ The people replied, "You are only humans like us, and the Most Compassionate has not revealed anything. You are simply lying!"

The people of Antioch refused to believe that they were messengers; that they were special or different in any way. They said you are not messengers; rather, "you are only humans like us." There is absolutely no difference between us. You are humans just like us; you eat what we eat, drink what we drink, and walk in the markets that we walk in. What makes you so special that Allah ﷻ chose you as messengers? The Most Merciful, Allah ﷻ, has not sent down anything. He has not sent down or revealed any commands or prohibitions. "You are simply lying" with respect to your claim. It is interesting to note that despite being polytheists, they still recognized the existence of Allah ﷻ and that He is al-Raḥmān. This is in contrast to the people of Quraysh; they also recognized the existence of Allah ﷻ but they claimed that they didn't know Him as al-Raḥmān.

The people of this town came up with three objections:

1. You cannot be messengers because you are human beings just like us,

2. There is no such thing as revelation, and

3. You are lying.

These are the same objections that were directed to all prophets, including our beloved Muḥammad ﷺ. Allah ﷻ tells us how the messengers responded.

قَالُـوا رَبُّنَا يَعْلَـمُ إِنَّـآ إِلَيْكُـمْ لَمُرْسَلُونَ ۝ وَمَـا عَلَيْنَـآ إِلَّا ٱلْبَلَـٰغُ ٱلْمُبِـينُ ۝

[16] The messengers responded, "Our Lord knows that we have truly been sent to you. [17] And our duty is only to deliver [the message] clearly."

The messengers responded to rejection and opposition with calmness and clarity. Although you think we are liars, our Lord knows that we have certainly been sent to you in order to invite you towards the truth and salvation. He ﷻ has definitely sent us to you and our job is simply to convey the message. We are not here to force, coerce, or compel anyone to accept the truth. We are simply delivering the message of God to you. Once you have the message, you can choose to do what you want with it. You are free to accept it or reject it, but you will be responsible for the decision that you make. The people of the town did not know how to respond to such a clear, simple, and straightforward message so they resorted to blame and threats.

قَالُوا إِنَّا تَطَيَّرْنَا بِكُمْ لَبِن لَّمْ تَنتَهُوا لَنَرْجُمَنَّكُمْ وَلَيَمَسَّنَّكُم مِّنَّا عَذَابٌ أَلِيمٌ ﴿١٨﴾

[18] The people replied, "We definitely see you as a bad omen for us. If you do not desist, we will certainly stone you ⌜to death⌝ and you will be touched with a painful punishment from us."

The people of the town accused the messengers of being some sort of bad omen. Idol worship and superstition go hand in hand. There is something about associating partners with Allah ﷻ and worshiping inanimate objects that causes further corruption of the fiṭrah and leads towards superstition. According to a few narrations, after the messengers arrived in Antioch, the town was afflicted with a severe drought. The people of the town blamed the messengers for the drought, saying that they brought bad luck and misfortune. They also thought they were bad luck because they were creating division and disunity in their society. This is very similar to what the leadership of Quraysh said to the Prophet ﷺ.

The people then threatened them. "If you do not desist, we will certainly stone you ⌜to death⌝ and you will be touched with a painful punishment from us." If you do not stop inviting towards Allah ﷻ and if you do not leave us alone, then we will stone you and punish you severely. It is interesting to see how falsehood is always aggressive, impatient, and violent. When falsehood, tyrants, oppressors, despots, and bullies are unable to respond intellectually, they resort to threats of physical violence and persecution. Again, the messenger responded in a cool, collected, and rational manner.

قَالُوا طَـٰٓئِرُكُم مَّعَكُمْ أَئِن ذُكِّرْتُم بَلْ أَنتُمْ قَوْمٌ مُّسْرِفُونَ ۝

¹⁹ The messengers said, "Your bad omen lies within yourselves. Are you saying this because you are reminded (of
the truth]? In fact, you are a transgressing people."

The messengers told them that the source and origin of their bad luck and misfortune is themselves. It is a result of their own actions, de-cisions, beliefs, and intentions. The reason for their misfortune and bad luck is disbelief and calling the messengers liars. The messengers then highlighted the absurdity of their comment. You think it is bad luck and mis-fortune when someone reminds you of Allah 🕮 and invites you to believe in Him? Bad luck or misfortune does not come because of our calling you to the way of Allah 🕮; rather, your bad luck is because you have passed the bound-aries and crossed the limits set by Allah 🕮.

As a result of crossing the boundaries and limits set by Allah 🕮, the peo-ple of the town began to persecute the messengers. They were stubborn and full of pride and arrogance. The person who they met at the outskirts of the town, Ḥabīb al-Najjār, heard about their persecution, so he came rushing to the town to help them.

وَجَآءَ مِنْ أَقْصَا ٱلْمَدِينَةِ رَجُلٌ يَسْعَىٰ قَالَ يَٰقَوْمِ ٱتَّبِعُوا ٱلْمُرْسَلِينَ ۝ ٱتَّبِعُوا مَن لَّا يَسْـَٔلُكُمْ أَجْرًا وَهُم مُّهْتَدُونَ ۝

[20] Then from the farthest end of the city a man came, rushing. He advised, "O my people! Follow the messengers. [21] Follow those who ask no reward of you, and are (rightly) guided.

After hearing that the messengers were being persecuted, Ḥabīb came rushing from the farthest part of the city to help and aid them. He advised his people with gentleness and kindness to follow the messengers who had been sent to guide them towards the truth and remove them from darkness to light. He advised them to follow the messengers because they are sincere and the proof of their sincerity is that they are not asking for anything in return for their efforts. They are not looking for wealth, money, power, influence, or authority. They are on the right path and have been guided to worship Allah ﷻ alone without any partners. Ḥabīb, coming to the defense of these messengers, was strange and suspicious. His people suspected that he had accepted their message and asked him with surprise, "Are you following their religion?" He responded with wisdom and words that were meant to penetrate their hearts.

وَمَا لِيَ لَآ أَعْبُدُ ٱلَّذِى فَطَرَنِى وَإِلَيْهِ تُرْجَعُونَ ۞ ءَأَتَّخِذُ مِن دُونِهِۦٓ ءَالِهَةً إِن يُرِدْنِ ٱلرَّحْمَـٰنُ بِضُرٍّ لَّا تُغْنِ عَنِّى شَفَـٰعَتُهُمْ شَيْـًٔا وَلَا يُنقِذُونِ ۞ إِنِّى إِذًا لَّفِى ضَلَـٰلٍ مُّبِينٍ ۞

²² And why should I not worship the One Who has originated me, and to Whom you will be returned. ²³ How could I take besides Him other gods whose intercession would not be of any benefit to me, nor could they save me if the Most Compassionate intended to harm me? ²⁴ Indeed, I would then be clearly astray.

He responded asking, "Why should I not?" Why should I not worship the One Who has created you and me, the entire universe and every single thing it contains, and the One to Whom you will be returned? Allah ﷻ alone is al-Fāṭir, the Originator, Who brought the universe into existence from nothing and the One to Whom everyone and everything will return on the Day of Judgment. al-Qurṭubī ﵀ mentions a unique linguistic point here, highlighting the eloquence and profundity of this statement. Ḥabīb attributes being originated by Allah ﷻ to himself because that is a blessing that results in gratitude, while he attributes resurrection to his people because, that is a warning that requires reflection. By doing so, he is expressing a sense of gratitude, while at the same time addressing the hearts of his people.

He continues by asking another rhetorical question, "How could I take besides Him other gods whose intercession would not be of any benefit to me, nor could they save me if the Most Compassionate intended to harm me?" How could I worship someone or something else whose intercession would be of no benefit whatsoever? They cannot even help themselves, so how are they going to help me? Why should I worship some inanimate object that cannot save me from any harm that the Most Compassionate may send my way? If Allah ﷻ, hypothetically speaking, were to send some sort of harm my way, these false deities would not be able to protect me or benefit me in any way, shape, or form. Again, the attribute of al-Raḥmān is being used, highlighting Allah's ﷻ infinite and limitless mercy. If I were to continue worshiping these idols and reject the call of the messengers then I would clearly be wrong. He then professed his faith openly, making them all witnesses to his belief in Allah ﷻ.

إِنِّىٓ ءَامَنتُ بِرَبِّكُمْ فَٱسْمَعُونِ ۝

25 I do believe in your Lord, so listen to me."

I have believed in your Lord. Him saying "your Lord" is significant. He says this to make them realize that Allah ﷻ is not just his Lord and the Lord of the messengers; He ﷻ is their Lord and the Lord of everything that exists. As soon as he said this, his own people attacked him. They started beating him and stoning him until he died. Even while he was being beaten he was asking Allah ﷻ to guide them. al-Suddiy ؓ says, "They stoned him while he was saying, 'O Allah, guide my people.'"[37] He had so much concern and care for his own people, and such a great desire for them to be guided, that he wished they would believe, even after they killed him. As soon as he

---

37 Qurṭubī, *al-Jāmiʿ li Aḥkām al-Quran*, 17:430

was martyred, Allah ﷻ granted him entry into Paradise.

قِيلَ ٱدْخُلِ ٱلْجَنَّةَ قَالَ يَٰلَيْتَ قَوْمِى يَعْلَمُونَ ۝ بِمَا غَفَرَ لِى رَبِّى وَجَعَلَنِى مِنَ ٱلْمُكْرَمِينَ ۝

[26] ⸢But they killed him, then⸣ he was told ⸢by the angels⸣, "Enter Paradise!" He said, "If only my people knew [27] of how my Lord has forgiven me, and made me one of the honorable."

Habīb al-Najjār was martyred while calling his people towards belief in Allah ﷻ and, as a result, Allah ﷻ granted him entry into Paradise. Qatādah ؓ said, "He was killed and admitted into Paradise where he is alive and being provided for."[38] As Allah ﷻ says in Sūrah Āl 'Imrān, "Never think of those martyred in the cause of Allah as dead. In fact, they are alive with their Lord, well provided for—rejoicing in Allah's bounties and being delighted for those yet to join them. There will be no fear for them, nor will they grieve."[39] Once he saw all of the rewards and blessings of belief, he expressed this genuine and sincere desire for his people to believe as well. He said, "If only my people knew of how my Lord has forgiven me, and made me one of the honorable." He felt that if his people knew of the reward and honor he received in the Hereafter, they would accept the truth.

---

38   Qurṭubī, *al-Jāmiʿ li Aḥkām al-Quran*, 17:430

39   وَلَا تَحْسَبَنَّ ٱلَّذِينَ قُتِلُوا فِى سَبِيلِ ٱللَّهِ أَمْوَاتًۢا بَلْ أَحْيَاءٌ عِندَ رَبِّهِمْ يُرْزَقُونَ * 3:169-170
فَرِحِينَ بِمَا آتَاهُمُ ٱللَّهُ مِن فَضْلِهِ وَيَسْتَبْشِرُونَ بِٱلَّذِينَ لَمْ يَلْحَقُوا بِهِم مِّنْ خَلْفِهِمْ أَلَّا خَوْفٌ عَلَيْهِمْ وَلَا هُمْ يَحْزَنُونَ

This genuine and sincere concern is the sign of a true, sincere, and righteous believer. He advised his people while he was alive and while he was "dead." A sincere believer wants good for every single human being. In this verse, Allah ﷻ highlights two distinct virtues of belief and martyrdom; forgiveness and honor. All of his sins, shortcomings, faults, and acts of disobedience were forgiven, and he was honored with the various blessings and favors of Paradise.

al-Qurṭubī ﷺ highlights a very important and profound lesson from this portion of the story. He writes, "There is great reminder in this verse and proof that it is necessary to control one's anger, have forbearance with the ignorant, be gracious with those who involve themselves with evil and injustice, strive hard to save them, be gentle, and not curse and supplicate against them. Don't you see how he hoped good for those who killed him, although they were unjust, non-believing idol-worshippers?"[40] After killing the three messengers and Ḥabīb, the people of this town were punished for their disbelief and their stubborn rejection of the truth.

۞ وَمَآ أَنزَلْنَا عَلَىٰ قَوْمِهِۦ مِنۢ بَعْدِهِۦ مِن جُندٍ مِّنَ ٱلسَّمَآءِ وَمَا كُنَّا مُنزِلِينَ ۝ إِن كَانَتْ إِلَّا صَيْحَةً وَٰحِدَةً فَإِذَا هُمْ خَٰمِدُونَ ۝

²⁸ We did not send any soldiers from the heavens against his people after his death, nor did We need to. ²⁹ All it took was one ˹mighty˺ blast, and they were extinguished at once.

---

40   Qurṭubī, al-Jāmiʿ li Aḥkām al-Quran, 17:433

Allah 🕌 did not send an army of Angels to destroy this particular town; they were destroyed by a single deafening cry. There was no need to send an army or soldiers to destroy them; Allah 🕌 in His infinite might and power had them destroyed with a single cry. Their destruction in such a manner highlights that they had no value in the eyes of Allah 🕌. Allah 🕌 commanded Jibrīl 🕊 to destroy them with a very powerful, piercing, and deadly cry.

يَـٰحَسْرَةً عَلَى ٱلْعِبَادِ مَا يَأْتِيهِم مِّن رَّسُولٍ إِلَّا كَانُوا بِهِۦ يَسْتَهْزِءُونَ ۝ أَلَمْ يَرَوْا كَمْ أَهْلَكْنَا قَبْلَهُم مِّنَ ٱلْقُرُونِ أَنَّهُمْ إِلَيْهِمْ لَا يَرْجِعُونَ ۝ وَإِن كُلٌّ لَّمَّا جَمِيعٌ لَّدَيْنَا مُحْضَرُونَ ۝

³⁰ Oh pity, such beings! No messenger ever came to them without being mocked. ³¹ Have the deniers not considered how many peoples We destroyed before them who never came back to life again? ³² Yet they will all be brought before Us.

Allah 🕌 is telling the non-believers, the ones who rejected the message, to feel and experience a severe sense of regret and loss. Ḥasrah is not just regret, but severe regret, bordering on a feeling of hopelessness. The cause of this feeling of regret and loss is their mockery of the messengers that led to their own destruction. "Oh pity, such beings!" can also be understood as an expression of amazement at the extreme injustice non-believers do to themselves and the punishment they will receive.

Allah 🕌 then highlights a common historical occurrence. "No messenger ever came to them without being mocked." This is a common thread that ties the stories of the majority of prophets and messengers together. The initial response of a community or people that was sent a prophet or messenger was always opposition and rejection. This gives us profound insight into the human condition; mankind is averse to change and reform. It is very difficult and challenging for people to change their beliefs, modify their practices, reform themselves, and change society. It is generally a gradual process that can be achieved through knowledge, wisdom, patience, and perseverance.

Allah ﷻ then poses a rhetorical question to those who deny the truth, "Have the deniers not considered how many peoples We destroyed before them who never came back to life again?" Through this rhetorical question, Allah ﷻ is encouraging the people of Quraysh and anyone who follows in their footsteps to reflect upon history. Reflect upon the history and punishment of past nations and communities that were completely destroyed because of their rejection and denial of the truth. This rhetorical question is also an indirect threat to the leadership of Quraysh. It is as if Allah ﷻ is telling them that if they continue their rejection and denial of the truth, then Allah ﷻ will punish them just as He ﷻ did these previous nations and communities.

Not only will they suffer destruction, disgrace, and humiliation in this world, but they will also be brought back to Allah ﷻ for judgment and recompense. "Yet they will all be brought before Us." On the Day of Judgment, Allah ﷻ will hold them accountable for their rejection of the truth, denial of the Messenger ﷺ, and injustice.

LESSONS AND BENEFITS FROM THE STORY OF THE PEOPLE OF THE TOWN

1.

The Importance of Examples - The story shows us a practical example of what was mentioned earlier in terms of belief and disbelief. Examples are powerful teaching tools that can be used to explain, clarify, and solidify ideas and concepts.

2.

Calling Towards the Truth - One of the most important responsibilties we have as conscious and concerned believers is to invite others towards the truth. Allah ﷻ has gifted us with the most valuable gift, īmān and Islam, and it is our respnsibility to share it with our families, friends, neighbors, co-workers, classmates, colleagues, and acquaintances. Inviting others towards belief in Allah ﷻ, His Messenger, and the Last Day should be done with sincerity, excellence, knowledge, wisdom, and gentleness. We should strive to be genuine in our speech and behavior. Inviting towards the truth can be both explicit and implicit, but it requires us to have pride and confidence in our faith, morals, customs, practices, and way of life.

3.

Help and Support for Good Causes - Allah's divine help and support is always with the righteous and their causes. The help of Allah ﷻ comes in several different shapes, sizes, and forms. Sometimes that help will be apparent and immediate, and at other times it may be discreet and delayed.

4.

Debating with Wisdom - A person inviting towards the truth will face impediements, roadblocks, and opposition. It is their responsibility to respond calmly with patience, forebearance, strength, and perseverence.

5.

Religious Persecution - Being persecuted, harassed, mocked, ridiculed, and made fun of is something that we have to accept and come to terms with. It's part of the package of being a firm and committed believer.

6.

Concern for One's Community

7.

Consolation and Comfort for the Believers

The next set of verses tells us about the beauty of Allah's creation through some of His āyāt, or signs. A sign is something that is used to provide information or directions. A sign can give instructions or provide directions towards one's destination. The signs of Allah ﷻ point us towards the direction of the Truth; towards the direction of the Divine. Everything around us, every created thing in this universe, is a sign of the existence, oneness, might, power, glory, magnificence, and omnipotence of Allah ﷻ. We can find the beauty, power, and magnificence of Allah ﷻ in every single thing that we see around us. Allah ﷻ draws our attention to these magnificent signs in several passages throughout the Quran. Sometimes we are directed towards the marvelous blue canopy above our heads, the sun, moon, and other celestial bodies. Sometimes our attention is directed towards the Earth and everything on it and within it; plants, trees, flowers, fruit, vegetation, grass, shrubs, streams, rivers, lakes, oceans, marine life, animals, insects, mountains, valleys, and minerals. Sometimes we are told to reflect upon ourselves and our humble origins. We are encouraged to use our minds; to think, ponder, and reflect upon these signs in order to recognize our Lord and Creator. Through this deep reflection and thought, we recognize, acknowledge, and affirm that He ﷻ truly is the Creator, Sustainer, and Nourisher of every single thing. Everything that we see, observe, and study in this world is a sign, proof, and evidence that Allah ﷻ exists and that He has the absolute power to do anything He wills. Several of these signs are also irrefutable proof of life after death and resurrection.

وَءَايَةٌ لَّهُمُ ٱلْأَرْضُ ٱلْمَيْتَةُ أَحْيَيْنَـٰهَا وَأَخْرَجْنَا مِنْهَا حَبًّا فَمِنْهُ يَأْكُلُونَ ۝ وَجَعَلْنَا فِيهَا جَنَّـٰتٍ مِّن نَّخِيلٍ وَأَعْنَـٰبٍ وَفَجَّرْنَا فِيهَا مِنَ ٱلْعُيُونِ ۝ لِيَأْكُلُوا مِن ثَمَرِهِۦ وَمَا عَمِلَتْهُ أَيْدِيهِمْ أَفَلَا يَشْكُرُونَ ۝ سُبْحَـٰنَ ٱلَّذِى خَلَقَ ٱلْأَزْوَٰجَ كُلَّهَا مِمَّا تُنۢبِتُ ٱلْأَرْضُ وَمِنْ أَنفُسِهِمْ وَمِمَّا لَا يَعْلَمُونَ ۝

³³ There is a sign for them in the dead earth: We give it life, producing grain from it for them to eat. ³⁴ And We have placed in it gardens of palm trees and grapevines, and caused springs to gush forth in it, ³⁵ so that they may eat from its fruit, which they had no hand in making. Will they not then give thanks? ³⁶ Glory be to the One Who created all ⌐things in⌐ pairs—⌐be it⌐ what the earth produces, their genders, or what they do not know!

This is a very powerful, beautiful, and profound set of verses highlighting several signs of Allah's absolute magnificence and power. The specific sign that's mentioned in this verse is one of the most direct, simple, logical, and observable proofs for the reality of life after death. Allah ﷻ is telling us that among the countless signs that point towards His existence and oneness, and His power and ability to bring the dead back to life, is giving life to dry, barren, and dead land. "There is a sign for them in the dead earth." Meaning, there is a sign for mankind in the dead earth that life after death is not only a possibility, it is a reality. "Dead earth" refers to a piece of land that is dry and barren; it has no plants, vegetation, or growth whatsoever.

Allah ﷻ then gives this "dead earth" life by sending down rain and causing all types of plants and vegetation to grow upon it. These plants are of different shapes, sizes, colors, heights, widths, and provide various benefits. This is a phenomenon that all of us as human beings have observed at some time or another. We are all familiar with a piece of land that is totally dry and barren. Then one night it rains, and all of a sudden, the following morning, that same dry and barren land is lush and green, bursting with life. Glory be to Allah ﷻ the Almighty the Majestic.

"We give it life, producing grain from it for them to eat." This dead earth is given life by Allah ﷻ, and, as a result, He produces grain from it for us to consume. Grain is referring to wheat and barley, the two most common grains consumed by human beings. It can also be referring to any type of grain that we eat as human beings.

"And We have placed in it gardens of palm trees and grapevines, and caused springs to gush forth in it, so that they may eat from its fruit..." Allah ﷻ is telling us that from this same dead earth, He produces gardens of palm trees and grapevines. Date palms and grapevines are mentioned specifically because, during the time of revelation, they were considered to be among the most valuable and best types of fruit. In order to sustain all this growth and vegetation, Allah ﷻ causes water in the form of rivers and springs to "gush forth in it." Water in the form of rivers and springs gush forth from the earth, providing continued life to all of these trees, vines, growth, and plants.

Allah ﷻ then tells us one of the reasons why He has gifted us with all these blessings and signs, "So that they may eat from its fruit." Allah ﷻ - our Lord, Creator, Sustainer, Provider, and Nourisher - set all of this in motion so that we can eat and benefit from the fruit. This is something profound and humbling to reflect upon; all of these amazing processes were created and set into motion for our own benefit; to provide us with sustenance.

Allah ﷻ then reminds us that we as human beings have no role whatsoever in the ultimate production of these grains, fruits, and sources of water. None of this was done through our own ability or capability. It was all done by Allah ﷻ. "Life is a miracle which no man can produce. It is God's hand that produces miracles, initiating life in what has been dead. The sight of growing plants, flowering gardens and ripening fruit should open people's eyes and hearts to appreciate the wonderful work engendered by God's hand. It splits the earth to allow the shoot to appear, longing for freedom and light, gives vigor to the stem which is eager to enjoy sunlight, loads the branches with leaves and fruit, opens up flowers and gets the fruit ready for picking, so that they may eat its fruit."[41] As human beings, we may till the land, plant the seeds, water them, and work the land, but we play no role whatsoever in the shoot breaking through the seed, then the earth, and gradually developing into a mature fruit producing plant.

Allah ﷻ concludes the verse with a rhetorical question that is meant as an instruction. "Will they not then give thanks?" After realizing, recognizing, and observing all of these amazing signs, will they not then give thanks? Meaning, be grateful to Allah ﷻ for all of these amazing things that He alone has created for our benefit, sustenance, and provision. Be grateful to Allah ﷻ for producing grains, trees, fruits, and water that are some of our main sources of nutrition and sustenance. Express gratitude to Allah ﷻ with the heart, tongue, and limbs through belief, submission, obedience, devotion, and servitude.

Allah ﷻ then reminds us that He is pure and free from any faults, and another sign of His existence, oneness, might, power, and perfection. "Glory be to the One Who created all ⌈things in⌉ pairs—⌈be it⌉ what the earth produces, their genders, or what they do not know!" Allah ﷻ declares His perfection because it is truly shocking and surprising that anyone would refuse to believe in Him or that someone would associate partners with Him after observing the irrefutable and undeniable proofs of His existence and oneness. In everyday language it is like saying in shock, "Really!?" After seeing all of the signs of Allah's existence and oneness, you still choose to disbelieve and reject the truth? Glory be to Allah ﷻ.

Allah ﷻ created everything in pairs. Here the word "azwāj" is translated as pairs, but a more accurate translation would be types. Allah ﷻ has created this universe and everything it contains with great diversity. In this verse He ﷻ highlights the diversity of plants, humans, and things we do not even know about; those things that we have not yet explored or discovered. He ﷻ has created plants in different shapes, sizes, and colors that serve various purposes. He created human beings as males and females with amazing diversity in terms of biology, psychology, and roles. Despite all of our advance-

---

41   Quṭb, *fī Ẓilāl al-Quran*, 5:2967

ments in science, technology, and medicine, there are so many things we still do not know. There are depths of the oceans that have not yet been explored and species of insects, animals, and birds that have not yet been discovered. There are things that exist that we have no clue about.

In the next few verses, Allah ﷻ mentions four signs that we observe above us in the sky that are related to time. First, He ﷻ mentions the alternation of night and day.

وَءَايَةٌ لَّهُمُ ٱلَّيۡلُ نَسۡلَخُ مِنۡهُ ٱلنَّهَارَ فَإِذَا هُم مُّظۡلِمُونَ ۝

³⁷ And a sign for them is the night. We strip (the cover of)
the day from it, and they are suddenly in darkness.

Another sign of the absolute power and oneness of Allah ﷻ is the creation of time through the alternation of night and day. Allah ﷻ peels away the light of the day, exposing the darkness of night. This is a very eloquent and illustrative way of describing how the day transitions into the night. It is as if the light is being peeled from the sky causing the darkness underneath it to be exposed. Then Allah ﷻ covers the darkness of night with the light of day. Materially speaking, the Earth revolving around its axis causes the alteration of night and day. Syed Quṭb writes, "The Quranic description here is unique as it shows the day intertwined with the night and then Allah strips the day off the night to let darkness spread. We may perhaps further appreciate the unique way the Quran uses to express this image when we remember how it actually happens. As the earth rotates facing the sun, every spot of it actually comes face to face with the sun when the day spreads over it. When the rotation of the earth changes and that spot no longer faces the sun, the day is stripped off it so as to plunge it into darkness. The same thing happens over every little part of the earth in progression, as if the light of day is pulled away or stripped to allow darkness to replace it. Thus the wording here accurately describes reality."[42]

The One Who created this universe and the systems that function within it, setting them in motion, controlling them, managing them, and sustaining them is Allah ﷻ and Allah ﷻ alone. The day transitioning into the night and the night transitioning back into the day is something that is observed by humans every single day in every single corner of the world. Despite its daily occurrence, it is a remarkable sign that deserves contemplation and thought. Anyone who reflects upon this sign with humility and sincerity will come to the conclusion that this is the design of the Almighty. Allah ﷻ then mentions the movement of the sun.

وَٱلشَّمْسُ تَجْرِى لِمُسْتَقَرٍّ لَّهَا ۚ ذَٰلِكَ تَقْدِيرُ ٱلْعَزِيزِ ٱلْعَلِيمِ ﴿٣٨﴾

[38] And the sun is quickly proceeding towards its destination. That is the designing of the Almighty, the All-Knowing.

Another sign of the absolute power, greatness, and oneness of Allah ﷻ is the sun and how it moves in its orbit. In this particular verse, Allah ﷻ is telling us that the sun is moving quickly towards its destination or resting place. The word mustaqarr is the passive participle from the verb istaqarra/yastaqirru, which means to come to rest, abide, or settle down. The word mustaqarr literally means a place of rest or a time of rest;

---

42   Quṭb, *fī Ẓilāl al-Quran*, 5:2968

meaning, mustaqarr can be related to time or space. That is why the mufassirūn have mentioned 2 possible meanings here:

1. The sun is moving quickly towards the end or destination of its journey, which is the Day of Judgment. That is why the verse has also been translated as, "The sun travels for its fixed term. That is the design of the Almighty, All-Knowing."

2. Others have said that the sun is moving towards its physical destination, which is under the throne of Allah ﷻ. Once the Prophet ﷺ asked Abū Dharr ؓ, "Do you know where the sun sets?" He replied, "Allah and His Messenger know best." He ﷺ said, "It travels till it prostrates itself underneath the throne and asks permission to rise again, and it is permitted. Then it is about to prostrate itself, but its prostration will not be accepted and it will ask permission to go on its course, but it will not be permitted and will instead be ordered to return where it came from. So it will rise in the West."[43] This is a phenomenon from the world of the unseen; it is something that cannot be seen or observed. There is no contradiction between this explanation of the Prophet ﷺ and modern science whatsoever.[44] Allah ﷻ is the Almighty, the All-Powerful, and can do as He wills. He simply says, "Be," and it is.

"That is the designing of the Almighty the All-Knowing," meaning Allah ﷻ is the One Who causes the alternation of night and day and the One Who has designed this particular course for the sun.

In these verses, Allah ﷻ has mentioned some examples of His absolute power and greatness, inviting us to reflect and ponder so that it will lead us to the only correct logical conclusion - that Allah ﷻ exists. One of the reasons for mentioning the sun specifically is to remind us that it is not moving on its own; the sun is not moving of its own volition or power. Instead, it is moving in subservience to the One who is Almighty and All-Knowing. It is moving under the predetermined system set by Allah ﷻ. It moves with the permission and will of Allah ﷻ. Every time the sun rises and every time it

---

43   Bukhārī, *k. al-tawḥīd, b. wa kāna ʿarshuhu ʿalā al-māʾ, wa huwa rabb al-ʿarsh al-ʿaẓīm,* 7424

44   For a more detailed discussion regarding this, please see *Ma'riful Quran.*

sets, it does so with the permission of Allah ﷻ.

Allah ﷻ then reminds us of another sign of His infinite might, power, and existence.

وَٱلْقَمَرَ قَدَّرْنَـٰهُ مَنَازِلَ حَتَّىٰ عَادَ كَٱلْعُرْجُونِ ٱلْقَدِيمِ ٣٩

³⁹ As for the moon, We have ordained ⸢precise⸣ phases for it, until it ends up like an old, curved palm stalk.

Allah ﷻ is now drawing our gaze and attention towards the moon and its various phases. Allah ﷻ has made specific phases through which the moon passes. The moon completes its orbit once a month. If the month is 30 days long, the moon is not seen for two nights. If it is 29 days, then the moon is not seen on one night. Therefore, the moon has 28 observable phases. "As the Moon orbits around Earth and Earth orbits around the Sun, the angle between the Sun, Moon, and Earth changes. As a result, the amount of sunlight that reflects off the Moon and travels to our eyes changes every day. (The Moon itself produces no light of its own.)

We see the Moon's disk change from all dark to all light to all dark again: This span of time is called a lunar cycle, lunation, lunar month, or synodic month. The length of the cycle can vary slightly, but on average, it is 29.53059 days.

Astronomers have broken down this cycle into four primary Moon phases: New Moon, First Quarter, Full Moon, and Last Quarter. There are also four secondary phases: Waxing Crescent, Waxing Gibbous, Waning Gibbous, and Waning Crescent. The primary phases occur at a specific moment, no matter where you are on Earth, which is then converted to local time.

(Depending on where you live, you may or may not be able to see the exact moment of a phase, in part because the Moon may not have risen yet in your area.) The secondary phases, however, represent a span of time rather than a specific moment."[45]

When the moon reaches its final stages of the month, it becomes smaller and smaller, delicate, turns yellow, and takes the shape of a crescent. "It ends up like an old, curved palm stalk," is referring to the waning crescent.

The moon is not passing through these phases by itself; rather, it is Allah ﷻ who has set this amazing system into place. Observing the moon on a nightly basis as it passes through these phases is a phenomenal way of connecting our hearts to the beauty and majesty of Allah ﷻ. At the beginning of the month, we observe the birth of the moon as a thin crescent. This thin crescent gradually increases in size, taking shape as a full moon near the middle of the month. The full moon then begins to decrease in size, returning to the shape of a thin crescent at the end of the month.

لَا ٱلشَّمْسُ يَنۢبَغِى لَهَآ أَن تُدْرِكَ ٱلْقَمَرَ وَلَا ٱلَّيْلُ سَابِقُ ٱلنَّهَارِ وَكُلٌّ فِى فَلَكٍ يَسْبَحُونَ ﴿٤٠﴾

[40] It is not for the sun to catch up with the moon, nor does the night outrun the day. Each is traveling in an orbit of their own.

---

45 *Moon phase calendar 2022: What's The moon phase today?* Almanac.com. (n.d.). Retrieved May 4, 2022, from https://www.almanac.com/astronomy/moon/calendar

In this verse, Allah ﷻ brings together the signs He mentioned in the previous verses; the sun, moon, night, and day. All of these are manifestations of Allah's infinite might, power, mercy, precision, and planning. This system that Allah ﷻ has set into motion is perfect, accurate, and precise and will continue to run its course until the end of time. The sun will not overtake the moon. We never see the sun rising in the middle of the night, nor do we see the moon manifest in the middle of the day. We also do not see night coming before the end of the day or the day coming before the end of the night. The night comes at its time and day comes at its time. ibn 'Abbās ﷺ says this means that when the sun rises, the moon has no light, and when the moon is illuminated, the sun has no light.[46] Mujāhid ﷺ says it means that the light of the sun does not resemble the light of the moon. [47]

All of these celestial bodies and signs are under the direct command of Allah ﷻ, and do exactly as they are commanded. Every single planet, every star, celestial body, the sun and the moon, are moving in their specified orbits. "Each one is floating in an orbit." The celestial bodies moving in their orbits are being compared to a body or ship moving through the sea.

Allah ﷻ then brings another sign and proof of His ultimate might, power, and magnificence. Just as He has given us the ability to move and travel across land, He has also given us the ability to move and travel across water.

وَءَايَةٌ لَّهُمْ أَنَّا حَمَلْنَا ذُرِّيَّتَهُمْ فِي ٱلْفُلْكِ ٱلْمَشْحُونِ ۝ وَخَلَقْنَا لَهُم مِّن مِّثْلِهِۦ مَا يَرْكَبُونَ ۝ وَإِن نَّشَأْ نُغْرِقْهُمْ فَلَا صَرِيخَ لَهُمْ وَلَا هُمْ يُنقَذُونَ ۝ إِلَّا رَحْمَةً مِّنَّا وَمَتَـٰعًا إِلَىٰ حِينٍ ۝

---

46   Qurṭubī, al-Jāmiʿ li Aḥkām al-Quran, 17:450

47   Qurṭubī, al-Jāmiʿ li Aḥkām al-Quran, 17:450

41 Another sign for them is that We carried their ancestors
[with Nūḥ ﷺ] in the fully loaded Ark, 42 and created for
them things similar to it on which they ride. 43 And if We
so will, We can drown them; then no one will respond to
their cry, nor will they be rescued, 44 except by mercy from
Us, allowing them enjoyment for a ˹little˺ while.

In this verse, Allah ﷻ is highlighting another sign of His existence, oneness, might, power, and glory. al-Qurṭubī ﷺ mentions that the sign
here contains a lesson, blessing, and warning. It is a lesson because all
signs contain lessons that we can derive and understand. It is a blessing because several signs are blessings of Allah ﷻ that He has bestowed upon us. It
is a warning because some signs are used to warn people of the consequences
of their choices and actions.[48]

Another sign, proof, and evidence of the existence and greatness of Allah
ﷻ is that He "carried their ancestors [with Nūḥ ﷺ] in the fully loaded Ark."
According to most tafsīr authorities, this is referring to Nūḥ's Ark through
which Allah ﷻ preserved all of humanity. That is why the translation has
"with Nūḥ ﷺ" in brackets. Another interpretation is that this could be referring to past generations being carried in the wombs of their mothers, which
are likened to a fully loaded ark.

A more general reading of the verse is that Allah ﷻ allows ships and
boats to stay afloat on top of oceans, seas, rivers, and all other bodies of water, which allows us to travel across them. Allah ﷻ in His infinite wisdom
has created the laws of nature in such a way that allow us to build and con-
struct ships out of wood, metal, and other materials of various sizes, shapes,
and weight that are able to float and travel across bodies of water of various
depths. This in and of itself is an amazing reality to reflect upon.

"And created for them things similar to it on which they ride." According
to most tafsīr authorities, this is referring to camels, which were known as
"the ships of the desert." This portion of the verse can also be understood
more generally as referring to various modes of transportation, including
camels, horses, other beasts, and in the modern era, cars, trains, and planes.

Allah ﷻ reminds us that these various modes of transportation across

---

48   Qurṭubī, *al-Jāmiʿ li Aḥkām al-Quran*, 17:452

land and sea are blessings and favors from Him upon us. They are part of Allah's infinite grace and mercy.

"And if We so will, We can drown them; then no one will respond to their cry, nor will they be rescued, except by mercy from Us, allowing them enjoyment for a ˹little˺ while." Through this reminder, Allah ﷻ is reminding us to have humility and to be grateful for His favors and blessings upon us. Despite the complex engineering behind the design of ships and the expertise of their crews, if Allah ﷻ wills, He could cause them to drown within the blink of an eye. At that moment of drowning there will be no one there to help them or rescue them. This is a powerful reminder of human fragility and that everything is truly in the hands of Allah ﷻ. It is through the grace and mercy of Allah ﷻ that He allows us to travel across the oceans, seas, and rivers. It is also through His grace and mercy that He allows us to live and enjoy life "for a little while." People who have experience traveling by sea are well aware of the various dangers posed by the water and weather.

In the next set of verses, Allah ﷻ tells us about the attitude of the non-believers when they are told to fear Allah ﷻ and reminded of the various and diverse signs of His existence, oneness, might, power, omnipotence, and glory. Despite witnessing, observing, and experiencing these various amazing signs, they ignore them out of pride, arrogance, ignorance, and stubbornness. There are locks on their hearts and covers over their eyes, preventing them from accepting and seeing the truth that is right in front of them.

وَإِذَا قِيـلَ لَهُـمُ ٱتَّقُـوا مَـا بَـيْنَ أَيْدِيكُـمْ وَمَـا خَلْفَكُـمْ لَعَلَّكُـمْ تُرْحَمُـونَ ۝ وَمَـا تَأْتِيهِـم مِّـنْ ءَايَـةٍ مِّـنْ ءَايَـٰتِ رَبِّهِـمْ إِلَّا كَانُـوا عَنْهَا مُعْرِضِـينَ ۝

⁴⁵ And [they pay no heed] when it is said to them, "Save yourselves from that (punishment) which is before you (in this world) and that which will come after you (die), so that you may receive mercy." ⁴⁶ Whenever a sign comes to them from their Lord, they turn away from it.

Allah ﷻ - in His infinite grace and mercy - sends warnings to those who wrong themselves through disbelief, ingratitude, and rejection of the truth. Allah ﷻ reminds them that they can still receive His grace and mercy if they pay attention and take lessons from the warnings sent through prophets, messengers, and scripture. When they are reminded to beware of the punishment that is before them in this world and the punishment that will befall them in the hereafter, they turn away and ignore it. They pay no attention to it whatsoever. According to several tafsīr authorities "that (punishment) which is before you" is referring to the previous nations that were destroyed because of their rejection of the truth and opposition to their respective prophets and messengers. "And that which will come after you" is referring to the punishment they will experience in the hereafter for their rejection of the truth.

They hear the warning with their ears, they see the consequences of rejecting the truth on their travels, yet it doesn't penetrate their hearts. "Whenever a sign comes to them from their Lord, they turn away from it." "Although all these signs are enough to cause an open heart to shudder and bring it in line with the universe, the unbelievers will not see them for what they are, and even if they do see them, they still do not reflect on them."[49] That is their attitude towards any sign or proof that calls them to believe in Allah ﷻ.

---

49   Quṭb, *fī Ẓilāl al-Quran*, 5:2971

VERSE 47

وَإِذَا قِيـــلَ لَهُـــمْ أَنفِقُـــوا مِمَّـــا رَزَقَكُـــمُ ٱللَّهُ قَـــالَ ٱلَّذِيـــنَ كَفَـــرُوا
لِلَّذِيـــنَ ءَامَنُـوٓا أَنُطْعِـــمُ مَـن لَّـوْ يَشَآءُ ٱللَّهُ أَطْعَمَـــهُۥٓ إِنْ أَنتُـمْ إِلَّا فِى
ضَلَـٰلٍ مُّبِـينٍ ۝

⁴⁷ And when it is said to them, "Donate from what Allah
has provided for you," the disbelievers say to the believers,
"Why should we feed those whom Allah could have fed if
He wanted to? You are clearly astray!"

Not only do they ignore the signs, reject the truth, and disbelieve,
but their hearts are also hard and blackened to such an extent that
they feel no sympathy or care for others. When they are asked to
spend in charity and help out the poor and needy, they make a mockery out
of it and sarcastically ask, "Why should we feed those whom Allah could have
fed if He wanted to?" This is obviously a ridiculous and outrageous statement, highlighting their arrogance, ignorance, and stinginess. This verse can
be seen as a severe criticism of stinginess and miserliness. On top of their
stinginess and miserliness, they had the audacity to claim that the Muslims
were wrong. "You are clearly astray" for asking us to give charity to the poor
and following the teachings of Muḥammad ﷺ.

al-Qurṭubī ؒ mentions the background in which this verse was revealed. Abū Bakr ؓ was extremely generous and charitable and he would
take care of the poor Muslims by giving them food and other provisions. One
day, Abū Jahl met him and said, "O Abū Bakr, do you believe that Allah is able
to feed these people?" He ؓ replied, "Yes." To which Abū Jahl replied, "So

why is it that He does not feed them?" He said, "He tests some people with poverty and others with wealth. As for the poor, they are told to be patient, and the wealthy are commanded to give." Abū Jahl replied, "O Abū Bakr, you are clearly astray. Do you believe that Allah is able to feed these people, yet He does not feed them, then you feed them?" In response, this particular verse was revealed.[50]

Abu Jahl's attitude was common among the enemies and opponents of the Prophet ﷺ. It highlights their ignorance of the deep divine wisdom in Allah's laws and how He organizes, manages, and controls the affairs of this world. Without a doubt, Allah ﷻ is al-Razzāq - the Provider - the One Who provides life, air, food, drink, clothes, and shelter to every single thing that exists in this universe. He ﷻ alone is the One Who provides for every single human being, but He provides for everyone in different ways, according to His divine knowledge, decree, wisdom, and plan. Syed Quṭb writes, "It is God's will that people should have needs which they cannot attain to without hard work, such as planting the earth, extracting its raw material to manufacture things, transporting its produce from place to place, offering such produce in return for other products or for money, etc. It is also His will that people differ in their talents and abilities to ensure that everything needed to fulfill man's task of building human life on earth is available. The accomplishment of this task not only needs talents and abilities that earn money and produce wealth; it also requires others that can meet different human needs, without earning money. This makes for a complex human society, in which people have different lots in a bustling world, and across generations. However, the resulting differences of the means available to different people does not lead to the ruination of life and society. In fact, it is a by-product of life's movement. Therefore, Islam addresses the individual, requiring those who have plenty to relinquish a portion of their money, which is given to the poor to provide for their food and other needs. By doing so, Islam reforms a great many people, rich and poor alike...Islam puts in place a system that ensures fair opportunities for everyone. It then allows varied human activities, which are necessary for the fulfillment of man's role on earth, to run their course. Furthermore, it deals with any negative side effects."[51]

The next set of verses deals with how the non-believers rejected the Day

---

50   Qurṭubī, *al-Jāmiʿ li Aḥkām al-Quran*, 17:458

51   Quṭb, *fī Ẓilāl al-Quran*, 5:2971

of Judgment. The non-believers of Quraysh had adopted an attitude of ridicule and mockery towards the concept of life after death. Allah ﷻ explains that life after death is an absolute certainty, it is the truth, and that it is going to happen without a doubt.

وَيَقُولُونَ مَتَىٰ هَٰذَا ٱلْوَعْدُ إِن كُنتُمْ صَٰدِقِينَ ۝ مَا يَنظُرُونَ
إِلَّا صَيْحَةً وَٰحِدَةً تَأْخُذُهُمْ وَهُمْ يَخِصِّمُونَ ۝ فَلَا يَسْتَطِيعُونَ
تَوْصِيَةً وَلَآ إِلَىٰ أَهْلِهِمْ يَرْجِعُونَ ۝

⁴⁸ And they say, "When will this promise come true, if you are truthful?" ⁴⁹ They are looking for nothing but for a single Cry that will seize them when they will be quarreling. ⁵⁰ So they will not be able to make a bequest, nor will they return to their household.

These verses serve as a source of consolation to the Prophet ﷺ as well as a veiled threat and warning to those who consciously choose to reject the truth and refuse to believe in the Hereafter. When they are advised to believe in Allah ﷻ, fear His punishment, and warned about the consequences of their disbelief in this world and the next, they ask mockingly, "When will this promise come true, if you are truthful?" This question is full of pride, arrogance, mockery, and ridicule. The non-believers of Makkah believed that they were untouchable. When the Prophet ﷺ would warn them about punishment in this world and the next, they would take it lightly and ask for the Prophet ﷺ to hasten it. If you are telling the truth, if we are going to be punished because of our beliefs and behavior, then where is the punishment?

Allah ﷻ Himself responds to their mockery and ridicule saying, "They are looking for nothing but for a single Cry that will seize them when they will be quarreling. So they will not be able to make a bequest, nor will they return to their household." There is nothing between them and the Day of Resurrection except for a single Cry. This single Cry is referring to the first blowing of the Trumpet by the Angel Isrāfīl. Isrāfīl has been commanded by Allah ﷻ to blow into the Trumpet at an appointed time that will signal the end of the life of this world. After the first sounding of the Trumpet, everybody and everything on the face of the earth will pass away and cease to exist. As Allah ﷻ says, "The Trumpet will be blown and all those in the heavens and all those on the earth will fall dead, except those Allah wills ⌐to spare⌐. Then it will be blown again and they will rise up at once, looking on ⌐in anticipation.⌐"[52]

Allah ﷻ describes the sudden and unexpected nature of the world coming to an end, saying that it "will seize them when they will be quarreling. So they will not be able to make a bequest, nor will they return to their household." The sound of the Trumpet will come upon them out of nowhere, all of a sudden. The end of this world, death, will come upon them suddenly while they are engaged in their normal everyday activities such as buying and selling, eating and drinking, talking and conversing, walking and driving. Abū Hurairah ؓ narrates that the Prophet ﷺ said, "The Hour will not be established till the sun rises from the west, and when it rises (from the west) and people see it, then all of them will believe (in Allah). But that will be the time when 'No good it will do to a soul to believe then. If it believed not before...'[53] The Hour will be established (so suddenly) that two persons spreading a garment between them will not be able to finish their bargain, nor will they be able to fold it up. The Hour will be established while a man is carrying the milk of his she-camel, but cannot drink it; and the Hour will be established when someone is not able to prepare the tank to water his livestock from it; and the Hour will be established when some of you has raised his food to his mouth but cannot eat it."[54] Allah ﷻ says it will come so fast and so suddenly

---

52 39:68 - وَنُفِخَ فِى الصُّورِ فَصَعِقَ مَن فِى السَّمَاوَاتِ وَمَن فِى الْأَرْضِ إِلَّا مَن شَاءَ اللَّهُ ثُمَّ نُفِخَ فِيهِ أُخْرَىٰ فَإِذَا هُمْ قِيَامٌ يَنظُرُونَ

53 6:158 - لَا يَنفَعُ نَفْسًا إِيمَانُهَا لَمْ تَكُنْ آمَنَتْ مِن قَبْلُ

54 Bukhārī, *k. al-riqāq, b. ṭulūʿ al-shams min al-maghrib*, 6506

that they will not have time to advise one another or return to their homes and families.

Allah ﷻ then tells us about the second sounding of the Trumpet, the one that will signal resurrection and bring everything back to life. There is a narration that tells us there is a period of forty years between each sounding of the Trumpet.

وَنُفِخَ فِي ٱلصُّورِ فَإِذَا هُم مِّنَ ٱلْأَجْدَاثِ إِلَىٰ رَبِّهِمْ يَنسِلُونَ ۝ قَالُوا يَٰوَيْلَنَا مَنۢ بَعَثَنَا مِن مَّرْقَدِنَا ۗ هَٰذَا مَا وَعَدَ ٱلرَّحْمَٰنُ وَصَدَقَ ٱلْمُرْسَلُونَ ۝ إِن كَانَتْ إِلَّا صَيْحَةً وَٰحِدَةً فَإِذَا هُمْ جَمِيعٌ لَّدَيْنَا مُحْضَرُونَ ۝

51 The Trumpet will be blown (a second time), then—behold!—they will rush from the graves to their Lord. 52 They will say, "Woe to us! Who has raised us from our place of rest? This must be what the Most Compassionate warned us of; the messengers told the truth!" 53 It will be no more than a single Cry, and in no time they will all be brought before Us.

The Trumpet will be sounded a second time by the Angel Isrāfīl signaling the beginning of resurrection. All of creation will be brought back to life, and every human being, from the beginning of time until the end of time, will rise from their graves. All of creation will rise from their graves and move quickly towards Allah ﷻ for the gathering and judgment. Allah ﷻ describes this in Sūrah al-Qamar saying, "They will come forth from the graves as if they were swarming locusts, rushing towards the caller."[55] Allah ﷻ also describes this event saying, "The Day they will come forth from the graves swiftly, as if racing to an idol [for a blessing]."[56]

As the non-believers rise from their graves, they will feel this immense sense of regret, remorse, and sorrow causing them to curse themselves. "Woe to us! Who has raised us from our place of rest? This must be what the Most Compassionate warned us of; the messengers told the truth!" This verse is capturing the magnitude of their remorse, regret, and shock. Wayl is a very powerful expression that conveys different shades of meaning. It is a word that is used to express great distress and sorrow. They will express this great distress and sorrow at the time of resurrection because they will know for sure that they were wrong. They will ask in a state of shock, confusion, and bewilderment, "Who has raised us from our place of rest? What's going on? Who has brought us back to life?"

It is interesting to note that they refer to their graves as a place of rest, even though they will have experienced punishment in the grave. As Muslims, we believe in the idea or concept of punishment in the grave. There are several verses of the Quran and aḥādīth of the Prophet ﷺ that establish this reality. What we learn from these verses and aḥādīth is that the graves of the non-believers will be turned into a pit from the pits of Hell. The graves of these individuals were definitely not a place of rest nor comfort. Their graves being a place of rest is relative. They refer to their graves as a place of rest because compared to the horrors and terrors that lie ahead of them, their graves were comfortable.

Once the initial shock of resurrection wears off, they will realize that this is the day they were warned about. "This must be what the Most Compassionate warned us of; the messengers told the truth!" Again, the word choice here is very unique and interesting. They will refer to Allah ﷻ by His attribute of mercy because they will recognize that it was through His infinite mercy that they were warned. They will realize that the prophets and messengers who had been sent to them were telling the truth, but obviously it will be too late.

Allah ﷻ then emphasizes how fast this will occur. "It will be no more than a single Cry, and in no time they will all be brought before Us." This sin-

---

55   يُخْرُجُونَ مِنَ الْأُجْدَاثِ كَأَنَّهُمْ جَرَادٌ مُّنتَشِرٌ * مُّهْطِعِينَ إِلَى الدَّاعِ - 54:7-8

56   يَوْمَ يُخْرُجُونَ مِنَ الْأُجْدَاثِ سِرَاعًا كَأَنَّهُمْ إِلَى نُصُبٍ يُوفِضُونَ - 70:43

gle Cry is referring to the second sounding of the Trumpet, which is known as nafkhah al-baʿth. All of creation will be gathered before Allah ﷻ for judgment and accounting with this single Cry. Allah ﷻ then reminds us that on that day we will experience ultimate justice.

فَٱلْيَوْمَ لَا تُظْلَمُ نَفْسٌ شَيْئًا وَلَا تُجْزَوْنَ إِلَّا مَا كُنتُمْ تَعْمَلُونَ ﴿٥٤﴾

⁵⁴ On that Day no soul will be wronged in the least, nor will
you be rewarded except for what you used to do.

The life of this world is full of injustice, oppression, and wrongdoing; the strong take advantage of the weak and the rich take advantage of the poor. On the Day of Resurrection, Allah ﷻ will establish ultimate justice. No person, animal, or being will be subject to even the least bit of injustice. Everybody will be recompensed according to their actions. Allah ﷻ will reward those who deserve it through His infinite grace and mercy and will hold those who deserve it accountable through His infinite justice.

There is a very beautiful and powerful ḥadīth qudsī that gives us greater insight into Allah's ﷻ infinite justice and mercy. It is narrated from Abū Dharr al-Ghifārī ﷺ from the Prophet ﷺ from his Lord, that He said: "O My servants! I have forbidden ẓulm (oppression) for Myself, and I have made it forbidden amongst you, so do not oppress one another. O My servants, all of you are astray except those whom I have guided, so seek guidance from Me and I shall guide you. O My servants, all of you are hungry except those whom I have fed, so seek food from Me and I shall feed you. O My servants, all of you are naked except those whom I have clothed, so seek clothing from Me and I shall clothe you. O My servants, you commit sins by day and by night, and I forgive all sins, so seek forgiveness from Me and I shall forgive you. O My servants, you will not attain harming Me so as to harm me, and you will not attain benefitting Me so as to benefit Me. O My servants, if the first of you and the last of you, and the humans of you and the jinn of you, were all as pious as the most pious heart of any individual amongst you, then this would not increase My Kingdom an iota. O My servants, if the first of you and the last of you, and the humans of you and the jinn of you, were all as wicked as the most wicked heart of any individual amongst you, then this would not decrease My Kingdom an iota. O My servants, if the first of you and the last of you, and the humans of you and the jinn of you, were all to stand together in one place and ask of Me, and I were to give everyone what he requested, then that would not decrease what I possess, except what is decreased of the ocean when a needle is dipped into it. O My servants, it is but your deeds that I account for you, and then recompense you for. So he who finds good, let him praise Allah, and he who finds other than that, let him blame no one but himself."[57]

Allah ﷻ is exalted and pure from committing any type of ẓulm by His essence. It is impossible and unimaginable that Allah ﷻ would do something that is unjust.

Generally ẓulm is defined as "putting something in the wrong place," violating another's right unjustly, or going beyond the limit. This does not occur with Allah ﷻ because He is the Owner and Lord of all creation and nothing has a right upon Him. That is why it is mentioned in numerous places throughout the Quran that Allah ﷻ does not wrong any soul. Allah ﷻ says, "And your Lord treats no one with injustice."[58] "Allah is not unjust even to the extent of the weight of an atom."[59] "Allah wills no injustice to the world."[60] It is clear that Allah ﷻ never has and never will commit any form of injustice. The ultimate and infinite justice of Allah ﷻ will be manifest on the Day of Judgment.

In the next few verses, Allah ﷻ describes some of the rewards, comfort, luxury, and pleasure that will be enjoyed by the people of Paradise. Those who believe and do righteous deeds will be admitted into gardens beneath

---

57   Muslim, *k. al-birr wa al-ṣilah wa al-ādāb, b. taḥrīm al-ẓulm*, 2577

58   وَلَا يَظْلِمُ رَبُّكَ أَحَدًا - 18:49

59   إِنَّ اللَّهَ لَا يَظْلِمُ مِثْقَالَ ذَرَّةٍ - 4:40

60   وَمَا اللَّهُ يُرِيدُ ظُلْمًا لِّلْعَالَمِينَ - 3:108

which rivers flow where they will reside for eternity enjoying rewards beyond human imagination.

إِنَّ أَصْحَـٰبَ ٱلْجَنَّـةِ ٱلْيَـوْمَ فِى شُـغُلٍ فَـٰكِهُونَ ۝ هُـمْ وَأَزْوَٰجُهُـمْ فِى ظِلَـٰلٍ عَلَى ٱلْأَرَآئِكِ مُتَّكِـُٔونَ ۝ لَهُـمْ فِيهَا فَـٰكِهَةٌ وَلَهُم مَّـا يَدَّعُونَ ۝ سَلَـٰمٌ قَوْلًا مِّـن رَّبٍّ رَّحِيـمٍ ۝

[55] Indeed, on that Day the residents of Paradise will be busy enjoying themselves. [56] They and their spouses will be in ⸢cool⸣ shade, reclining on ⸢canopied⸣ couches. [57] There they will have fruits and whatever they desire. [58] And "Peace!" will be ⸢their⸣ greeting from the Merciful Lord.

Allah ﷻ is painting an image of Paradise. He ﷻ is telling us that the residents of Paradise will be busy enjoying themselves. They will be busy enjoying the various comforts, luxuries, and pleasures of Paradise, which no eye has ever seen, no ear has ever heard, and which no one has even imagined. The residents of Paradise will not be enjoying these blessings by themselves; rather, they will be accompanied by their spouses. "They and their spouses will be in ⸢cool⸣ shade, reclining on ⸢canopied⸣ couches." They will be under the shade of the trees of Paradise experiencing a type of comfort and coolness that cannot be described in words. Although there is no comparison between this world and the next, comfort and coolness are things that we are familiar with and look forward to. Imagine a hot summer day with the rays of the sun beating down upon us. The shade and coolness provided by a large mature tree on a hot summer day is indescribable. It brings immediate comfort and relief from the heat of the sun.

They will be reclining with their spouses on canopied couches resting and relaxing. Allah ﷻ is painting an image of total and complete comfort and relaxation. Again, there is no real comparison between Paradise and the life of this world. However, after a long tiring day of work, stress, anxiety, meeting deadlines, and sitting in traffic, one of the things we look forward to is getting home and relaxing on a recliner. The residents of Paradise will be content and at peace.

"There they will have fruits and whatever they desire." During the time of revelation, fruits were consumed for enjoyment and pleasure. Allah ﷻ is telling us that the residents of Paradise will receive the various fruits of Paradise, which according to several aḥādīth of the Prophet ﷺ, are far superior to the fruits of this world. The residents of Paradise will also be granted and given whatever they desire. Anything they want will be given to them immediately; instant gratification. As Allah ﷻ says, "Surely those who say, 'Our Lord is Allah,' and then remain steadfast, the angels descend upon them, [saying,] 'Do not fear, nor grieve. Rather, rejoice in the good news of Paradise, which you have been promised. We are your supporters in this worldly life and in the Hereafter. There you will have whatever your souls desire, and there you will have whatever you ask for: as a welcoming gift from the Most Forgiving, Most Merciful One.'"[61]

"And 'Peace!' will be ⌜their⌝ greeting from the Merciful Lord." On top of all of the pleasures, rewards, and blessings of Paradise, Allah ﷻ Himself will greet the residents of Jannah with salām - safety, security, peace, and well-being - as the greatest gift of Paradise. The greatest reward bestowed on the residents of Paradise is the opportunity to gaze upon the Divine, which in the books of theology is termed the beatific vision. Jābir ؓ narrates that the Prophet ﷺ said, "While the people of Paradise are in their bliss, a light shines upon them. Then they lift their heads, and it is Allah ﷻ beholding them from above. Then He ﷻ says, 'Peace be upon you, O people of the Garden.' And that is the meaning of His saying, 'Peace, will be their greeting from the Merciful Lord.' So He looks at them and they look at Him, and they are not distracted by anything from that bliss so long as they are looking

---

61   41:30-32 - إِنَّ الَّذِينَ قَالُوا رَبُّنَا اللّٰه ثُمَّ اسْتَقَامُوا تَتَنَزَّلُ عَلَيْهِمُ الْمَلَائِكَةُ أَلَّا تَخَافُوا وَلَا تَحْزَنُوا وَأَبْشِرُوا بِالْجَنَّةِ الَّتِي كُنْتُمْ تُوعَدُونَ * نَحْنُ أَوْلِيَاؤُكُمْ فِي الْحَيَاةِ الدُّنْيَا وَفِي الْآخِرَةِ وَلَكُمْ فِيهَا مَا تَشْتَهِي أَنفُسُكُمْ وَلَكُمْ فِيهَا مَا تَدَّعُونَ * نُزُلًا مِّنْ غَفُورٍ رَّحِيمٍ

upon Him, until He is unveiled to them and His light and His blessing remain upon them in their abodes."[62] Allah  also says, "Their greeting on the Day they meet Him will be, 'Peace!' And He has prepared for them an honorable reward."[63]

After briefly describing some of the rewards and comforts of Paradise, Allah now describes some of the terrors awaiting the non-believers in the Hereafter. Part of the unique style of the Quran is that whenever there is some mention of belief, reward, and paradise, it will be followed by a mention of disbelief, punishment, and the fire. That is one of the reasons why after mentioning the rewards of the resident of Paradise, Allah immediately mentions the punishment of the mujrimūn (criminals).

This style of tarhīb (intimidating to stop bad) and targhīb (giving encouragement to do good) is very common throughout the Quran. It is used to create both a sense of fear and a sense of hope. A true believer lives their life in this world between fear of Allah's punishment and hope in His divine mercy. A true believer fears the Day of Judgment, standing before Allah, and being held accountable for their deeds and statement; they fear punishment and Allah's anger. This feeling of fear is not supposed to lead to a sense of hopelessness or despair. Rather, it should motivate us to work hard and struggle to obey the commandments of Allah and stay away from His prohibitions. At the same time we are supposed to have hope in the divine mercy, forgiveness, and grace of Allah. As believers we live our lives oscillating between the states of hope and fear, and that is the reality of īmān.

وَٱمْتَـٰزُوا ٱلْيَوْمَ أَيُّهَا ٱلْمُجْرِمُونَ ۝

---

62   Qurṭubī, al-Jāmiʿ li Aḥkām al-Qur'an, 17:471

63   تَحِيَّتُهُمْ يَوْمَ يَلْقَوْنَهُ سَلَامٌ وَأَعَدَّ لَهُمْ أَجْرًا كَرِيمًا - 33:44

⁵⁴ ⸢Then the disbelievers will be told,⸣ "Separate yourselves this Day, O guilty ones!

On the Day of Judgment the guilty ones - those guilty of disbelief, consciously rejecting the truth, and opposing the messengers - will be told to separate themselves from the believers. They will be told to separate themselves from the believers when they are standing on the Plain of Resurrection waiting for judgment to commence. That is one of the reasons why the Day of Judgment is also known as the Day of Division, Yawm al-Faṣl. Allah ﷻ then tells us why they will be told to separate themselves by mentioning what they are guilty of.

أَلَمْ أَعْهَدْ إِلَيْكُمْ يَـٰبَنِىٓ ءَادَمَ أَن لَّا تَعْبُدُوا ٱلشَّيْطَـٰنَ إِنَّهُۥ لَكُمْ عَدُوٌّ مُّبِينٌ ۝ وَأَنِ ٱعْبُدُونِى هَـٰذَا صِرَٰطٌ مُّسْتَقِيمٌ ۝

⁶⁰ Did I not command you, O Children of Adam, not to follow Satan, for he is truly your sworn enemy, ⁶¹ but to worship Me [alone]? This is the Straight Path.

Allah ﷻ is posing this rhetorical question as a way of scolding, reprimanding, and chiding the mujrimūn. Did I not advise you, command you, and warn you through my prophets and messengers to not follow Satan? Did I not warn you that Satan has been your open and sworn enemy since the beginning of your creation? I had commanded you in the world and reminded you over and over to believe in Me and worship Me alone. Worshiping Allah ﷻ alone without any partners is the Straight Path, the way of life that leads directly towards forgiveness, pardon, grace, mercy, success in this world, and salvation in the next. The path of belief, tawḥīd, submission, obedience, devotion, servitude, and the way of the prophets and messengers is the Straight Path. The Straight Path is referring to the way of life of Islam. Despite these clear warnings, Satan succeeded in leading many people away from the Straight Path.

وَلَقَدْ أَضَلَّ مِنكُمْ جِبِلًّا كَثِيرًا ۖ أَفَلَمْ تَكُونُوا تَعْقِلُونَ ۝

⁶² He had misguided many people from amongst you. So, did you not have sense?

Satan has succeeded in leading many people astray. He has succeeded in turning people away from the truth through his deception, tricks, lies, plots, and plans. He makes the bad seem good and leads people to fall prey to their wants and desires. He makes it seem like the enjoyment and pleasures of this world are worth it. He tricks people into sacrificing everlasting bliss and happiness for temporary fleeting moments of enjoyment and pleasure. "So, did you not have sense?" Were you not able to recognize his tricks, deception, and plots? Did you not understand that he is your open and sworn enemy? Did you not know that his mission is to take as many people as possible with him to the Fire?

هَـٰذِهِۦ جَهَنَّمُ ٱلَّتِى كُنتُمْ تُوعَدُونَ ۝ ٱصْلَوْهَا ٱلْيَوْمَ بِمَا كُنتُمْ تَكْفُرُونَ ۝

⁶³ This is the Hell you were warned of. ⁶⁴ Enter it today for your disbelief."

Allah ﷻ is informing us about the final destination of those people who consciously chose to disbelieve and reject the call of the messengers. It is the final destination of those who consciously chose to turn away from the truth and disobey Allah ﷻ. Not only were they warned about the punishment of Hellfire, but they were repeatedly warned about it through prophets and messengers. They were given enough time and opportunity to ponder over the message and accept it.

On the Day of Judgment, Allah ﷻ will scold and reprimand the mujrimūn saying, "This is the Hell you were warned of. Enter it today for your disbelief." This is the fire that you were told about during your lives. The same fire that I warned you about through My prophets and messengers. The same fire that you refused to believe in. On that Day, they will be shown the fire before being commanded to enter it. Allah ﷻ will command them to enter into the fire and taste and feel its heat and severity. In other words, these verses say, "This is the Fire the prophets and messengers warned you about, but you refused to listen. Now, taste the punishment of the Fire you used to deny!"

Abū Hurairah ﷺ narrates that the Messenger of Allah ﷺ said, "On the Day of Judgment, Allah ﷻ will gather mankind and jinn - the first and the last - on one plain...A caller will announce, 'This is the Hell you were warned of. Enter it today for your disbelief.' That is when nations will fall down on their knees, every nursing mother will abandon what she is nursing, every pregnant woman will deliver her burden ⌜prematurely,⌝ and you will see peo-ple ⌜as if they were⌝ drunk, though they will not be drunk; but the torment of Allah is ⌜terribly⌝ severe."[64]

On the Day of Judgment, no one will be able to make excuses and conceal their sins with lies and deception.

ٱلۡيَوۡمَ نَخۡتِمُ عَلَىٰٓ أَفۡوَٰهِهِمۡ وَتُكَلِّمُنَآ أَيۡدِيهِمۡ وَتَشۡهَدُ أَرۡجُلُهُم بِمَا كَانُوا۟ يَكۡسِبُونَ ۝

[65] On this Day We will seal their mouths, their hands will speak to Us, and their feet will testify to what they used to commit.

Allah ﷻ is describing a very frightening and terrifying scene from the Day of Judgment. This is a vivid scene that should really scare anyone who even thinks about doing something wrong, looking at something wrong, listening to something wrong, or saying something wrong.

On the Day of Judgment, no one will be able to make any excuses for their speech or behavior in front of Allah ﷻ. No one will be able to hide or conceal their sins and acts of disobedience. A person will not be able to deny anything they have done. "On this Day We will seal their mouths, their hands will speak to Us, and their feet will testify to what they used to com-

---

64   Qurṭubī, *al-Jāmiʿ li Aḥkām al-Quran*, 17:474

mit." A seal will be placed on our mouths, preventing us from speaking and our own limbs will testify against us. Allah ﷻ says in Sūrah al-Nūr, "On the Day their tongues, hands, and feet will testify against them for what they used to do. On that Day, Allah will give them their just penalty in full, and they will ⸢come to⸣ know that Allah ⸢alone⸣ is the Ultimate Truth."[65] In Sūrah Fuṣṣilat, Allah ﷻ says, "When they reach it, their ears, eyes, and skin will testify against what they used to do. They will ask their skin (furiously), 'Why have you testified against us?' It will say, 'We have been made to speak by Allah, Who causes all things to speak. He (is the One Who) created you the first time, and to Him you were bound to return. You did not (bother to) hide yourselves from your ears, eyes, and skin to prevent them from testifying against you. Rather, you assumed that Allah did not know much of what you used to do. It was that (false) assumption you entertained about your Lord that has brought about your doom, so you have become losers.'"[66]

Anas ﷺ narrates that, one day, while they were with the Messenger of Allah ﷺ, he laughed and asked, "Do you know why I'm laughing?" We replied, "Allah and His Messenger know best." He said, "At what a servant says to his Lord. He says, 'O Lord will you not protect me from injustice?' He replies, 'Of course.' He says, 'I will not accept any witness against myself but myself.' Allah ﷻ responds, 'Today your soul suffices as a witness against you, as do the noble scribes.' Then his mouth will be sealed and it will be said to his limbs, 'Speak!' So they will speak of his deeds. Then he will be permitted to speak and will say to his limbs, 'Away with you! Be doomed! It was on your behalf that I contended.'"[67]

In the life of this world, when we do something wrong or something we are ashamed of, we are able to hide it and make excuses. We usually do not want people to find out about what we have done, and if they do we will make excuses or try to justify it in some way. On the Day of Judgment, this will not be possible. Our own limbs - our hands, feet, skin, and tongues - will

---

65   24:24-25 - يَوْمَئِذٍ * يَعْمَلُونَ كَانُوا بِمَا وَأَرْجُلُهُم وَأَيْدِيهِمْ أَلْسِنَتُهُمْ عَلَيْهِمْ تَشْهَدُ يَوْمَ
يُوَفِّيهِمُ اللَّهُ دِينَهُمُ الْحَقَّ وَيَعْلَمُونَ أَنَّ اللَّهَ هُوَ الْحَقُّ الْمُبِينُ

66   41:20-23 - حَتَّى إِذَا مَا جَاءُوهَا شَهِدَ عَلَيْهِمْ سَمْعُهُمْ وَأَبْصَارُهُمْ وَجُلُودُهُم بِمَا كَانُوا
يَعْمَلُونَ * وَقَالُوا لِجُلُودِهِمْ لِمَ شَهِدتُّمْ عَلَيْنَا قَالُوا أَنطَقَنَا اللَّهُ الَّذِي أَنطَقَ كُلَّ شَيْءٍ وَهُوَ خَلَقَكُمْ أَوَّلَ
مَرَّةٍ وَإِلَيْهِ تُرْجَعُونَ * وَمَا كُنتُمْ تَسْتَتِرُونَ أَن يَشْهَدَ عَلَيْكُمْ سَمْعُكُمْ وَلَا أَبْصَارُكُمْ وَلَا جُلُودُكُمْ
وَلَكِن ظَنَنتُمْ أَنَّ اللَّهَ لَا يَعْلَمُ كَثِيرًا مِّمَّا تَعْمَلُونَ * وَذَلِكُمْ ظَنُّكُمُ الَّذِي ظَنَنتُم بِرَبِّكُمْ أَرْدَاكُمْ
فَأَصْبَحْتُم مِّنَ الْخَاسِرِينَ

67   Muslim, k. al-zuh wa al-raqā'iq, 2969

testify against us.

Allah ﷻ then clarifies some of the manifestations of His ultimate power over the non-believers.

VERSE 66

وَلَوْ نَشَآءُ لَطَمَسْنَا عَلَىٰٓ أَعْيُنِهِمْ فَٱسْتَبَقُوا ٱلصِّرَٰطَ فَأَنَّىٰ يُبْصِرُونَ ٦٦

⁶⁶ If We so will, We would wipe out their eyes (right here in this world), and they would be racing towards the way, but how would they see?

In this verse, Allah ﷻ is telling us that if He willed or if He wanted to, He could have made the non-believers physically blind in the life of this world. They would not be able to see anything, and as a result would be falling and stumbling, unable to reach their destination without help or assistance. But, out of His infinite and limitless mercy, He chose not to, so that they have the opportunity to use their eyesight to reflect and ponder upon the oneness of Allah ﷻ. Allah ﷻ is delivering this as a veiled threat and warning in order to create a sense of urgency within the non-believers of Makkah. Those who reject the truth and oppose the messengers will definitely be held accountable in the Hereafter. If Allah ﷻ wanted, He could hasten the punishment and hold them accountable right here in the life of this world by causing them to go blind. And once they are blinded, "how would they see?" Allah ﷻ continues with the veiled threat and warning.

وَلَوْ نَشَآءُ لَمَسَخْنَـٰهُمْ عَلَىٰ مَكَانَتِهِمْ فَمَا ٱسْتَطَـٰعُوا مُضِيًّا وَلَا يَرْجِعُونَ ۝

⁶⁷ And had We willed, We could have transfigured them on the spot, so they could neither progress forward nor turn back.

If Allah ﷻ willed, He could have disfigured the non-believers, changed their creation, and transformed them into pigs, monkeys, rocks or anything else. According to ibn ʿAbbās ﵂ this means that if Allah ﷻ willed, He could destroy them immediately in their homes. Again, Allah ﷻ did not do so out of His infinite and limitless mercy. Despite their rejection of the truth, opposition of the Messenger, arrogance, and pride, Allah ﷻ gave them the opportunity to rectify and change their ways.

In the next verse, Allah ﷻ warns the non-believers about wasting the opportunity granted to them. He ﷻ warns them about wasting their life and particularly their youth. By extension, it is a reminder for us as believers to value time and take advantage of our youth.

وَمَن نُّعَمِّرْهُ نُنَكِّسْهُ فِي ٱلْخَلْقِ ۚ أَفَلَا يَعْقِلُونَ ٦٨

68 And whoever We grant a long life, We reverse them in development. Will they not then understand?

Allah ﷻ is telling us that those people who have been blessed with long lives are returned to weakness after strength, inability after capability, and confusion after clarity. Allah ﷻ creates us weak as infants and children, in need of care and protection from our parents. He ﷻ then gives us strength, power, and ability as adolescents and adults, allowing us to navigate through life. He ﷻ then slowly brings us back to a state of weakness, frailty, and vulnerability in our old age. This is the system, design, and plan of Allah ﷻ. Allah ﷻ says in Sūrah al-Rūm, "It is God who creates you weak, then gives you strength, then weakness after strength, together with your gray hair: He creates what He wills; He is the All Knowing, the All Powerful."[68]

In this one verse, Allah ﷻ captures the entire cycle of human life on this earth; "It is God who creates you weak, then gives you strength, then weakness after strength, together with your gray hair." Allah ﷻ created us as human beings in a way that highlights His absolute power, magnificence, and glory. Allah ﷻ brings us into this world in a state of weakness. We are born into this world as weak and innocent beings without any physical, mental, or spiritual strength. As babies, infants, and toddlers, we are totally dependent on our parents and caretakers. They provide us food, drink, clothing, shelter, and nurture. Initially, we cannot even move on our own. Then slowly with

68   30:54 - الله الَّذِى خَلَقَكُم مِّن ضَعْفٍ ثُمَّ جَعَلَ مِن بَعْدِ ضَعْفٍ قُوَّةً ثُمَّ جَعَلَ مِن بَعْدِ

قُوَّةٍ ضَعْفًا وَشَيْبَةً يَخْلُقُ مَا يَشَاءُ وَهُوَ الْعَلِيمُ الْقَدِيرُ

time our strength increases; we start crawling, then walking, and eventually running. Initially, we are unable to speak and communicate; then it slowly develops over time. The same thing goes for all of our faculties, senses, and strengths. We grow and develop from an infant, to a toddler, to a child, and finally to an adult. This is what Allah ﷻ refers to as "strength." Then we continue to grow in our strength and abilities, our intellect, skills, physical, emotional, and spiritual strength until the age of 40. We reach the pinnacle of our strength and faculties at the age of 40, and then start to plateau. Then we slowly start to grow weak, feeble, frail, and old. Our strength starts to decline, our hair turns gray, our skin wrinkles, our bones become brittle, and our memory starts to fade. This is what Allah ﷻ refers to as "then weakness after strength, together with your gray hair." Here in Sūrah YāSīn, Allah ﷻ describes it as, "We reverse them in development." We start regressing and moving backwards in terms of our intellect, skills, and strength.

This cycle of life, from weakness to strength and then back to weakness, is a sign of Allah's unique and majestic might and power. It is a stark and powerful reality of the life of this world. Syed Quṭb writes, "No one escapes these stages. They never fail to affect anyone who survives; nor are they ever slow so as to come later than usual. These stages confirm that mankind is subject to a greater will that creates and determines as it pleases. That is the will of God who determines the age, life and stages of every creature in accordance with perfect knowledge and elaborate planning."[69]

After reminding us of the cycle of life, Allah ﷻ rhetorically asks, "Will they not then understand?" Do they not realize that as they get older, they become weaker and weaker and are able to do less and less? Do they not realize that Allah ﷻ has given them enough time, ample opportunity to research, and the ability to reflect, think, and arrive at the only logical conclusion?

This is also a reminder for us as Muslims to take advantage of our health and time. Time and good health are very precious, valuable, and limited commodities, and no one knows how much of it they have. Death can literally call upon them at any time, unexpectedly. Oftentimes, these two blessings are taken for granted and end up being under-utilized or even wasted. The Prophet ﷺ said, "There are two blessings that most people are deceived by;

---

69   Quṭb, fī Ẓilāl al-Quran, 5:2973

good health and free time."[70] The Prophet ﷺ also advised his companions, "Take advantage of five before five; youth before old age, health before illness, wealth before poverty, free time before becoming occupied, and life before death."[71]

In the next set of verses, Allah ﷻ again reminds us of His existence and oneness and explains the traits and qualities of messengership. The Sūrah revisits the themes and concepts it discussed earlier in a very powerful and eloquent way. The overall aim and objective is to show how Allah ﷻ is in absolute control of every single thing.

VERSE 69

وَمَا عَلَّمْنَـٰهُ ٱلشِّعْرَ وَمَا يَنۢبَغِى لَهُۥٓ إِنْ هُوَ إِلَّا ذِكْرٌ وَقُرْءَانٌ مُّبِينٌ ﴿٦٩﴾

[69] We did not teach him (the Prophet) poetry, and it is not proper for him. It is nothing (of that sort,) but (it is) an advice and a clear book that explains (the Truth),

With this verse, Allah ﷻ is rejecting some of the false accusations of the non-believers of Makkah. During the early days of the mission, when the Prophet ﷺ would recite Quran to them they would accuse him of being a poet and say what he is reciting is poetry. Allah ﷻ Himself is rejecting this false claim and saying He did not teach his Prophet ﷺ poetry. On top of that, the Prophet ﷺ was unlettered before receiving

---

70   Bukhārī, k. al-Riqāq, b. Mā jā'a fī al-riqāq wa an lā 'aysh illah 'aysh al-ākhirah, 6412

71   al-Bayhaqī, Shu'ab al-Īmān, 7:3319

revelation; he could not read or write. Allah ﷻ says, "You ˹O Prophet˺ could not read any writing ˹even˺ before this ˹revelation,˺ nor could you write at all. Otherwise, the people of falsehood would have been suspicious."[72] The Prophet ﷺ did not attend any school or university and did not receive any formal education; he also was not known for composing poetry or any other type of literature. If he was, then the Quraysh could have used that as a means to doubt the authorship of the Quran. They could have objected and said that these words that you are reciting are your own or that you learned it from previous scriptures and people. But they themselves knew without a doubt that the Prophet ﷺ was unlettered and that this was impossible. The greatest poets of his time acknowledged that the Quran was definitely not poetry; that it had to be divine in nature. For example, Unais ؓ, who himself was a poet, said, "I also compared his words to the verses of poets but such words cannot be uttered by any poet. By Allah, he is truthful and they are liars."[73]

On a side note, some ignorant individuals may misunderstand this as a critique of learning poetry, writing, composition, and education in general. It is extremely important to understand that learning beneficial knowledge is one of the most essential teachings of Islam. There is nothing inherently wrong with writing and poetry. They are amazing tools of communication and education that can be used for both good and bad. If they are being used for good, then they are praiseworthy, and if they are being used for bad, then they are blameworthy.

It is narrated that al-Ma'mūn said to Abū ʿAlī al-Minqarī, "It is been brought to my attention that you are unlettered, can't compose poetry, and make mistakes in pronunciation." He responded, "O leader of the believers! As for the mistakes in pronunciation, then perhaps my tongue slips at times. As for being unlettered and being unable to compose poetry, then the Prophet ﷺ also didn't write and compose poetry." Al-Ma'mūn said, "I asked you about three faults that you have and you introduced me to a fourth; ignorance! O ignorant fool! That was a virtue for the Prophet ﷺ and for you it is a shortcoming. The Prophet ﷺ was unlettered as part of proving his prophethood not because of some inherent fault in poetry and writing."[74]

---

72   وَمَا كُنتَ تَتْلُو مِن قَبْلِهِ مِن كِتَابٍ وَلَا تَخُطُّهُ بِيَمِينِكَ ۖ إِذًا لَّارْتَابَ الْمُبْطِلُونَ - 29:48

73   Muslim, *k. faḍā'il al-ṣaḥābah, b. min faḍā'il abī dharr*, 2473

74   Qurṭubī, *al-Jāmiʿ li Aḥkām al-Quran*, 17:485

Despite knowing that the Prophet ﷺ was unlettered, the leaders of Quraysh, in their desperation, still accused him of being a poet. In this one verse, Allah ﷻ is stating in absolute and unequivocal terms that the Prophet ﷺ is not a poet and that the Quran is not poetry. Rather, what the Prophet ﷺ is conveying is "only a Reminder and a clear Quran." The Quran is a very powerful and profound reminder guiding people towards belief, goodness, righteousness, and righteous deeds. It is a clear book, easy to understand, reflect upon, and implement.

Allah ﷻ then tells us about one of the main roles of the Quran and the Prophet ﷺ himself.

لِّيُنذِرَ مَن كَانَ حَيًّا وَيَحِقَّ ٱلْقَوْلُ عَلَى ٱلْكَٰفِرِينَ ۝

70 to warn whoever is (truly) alive and fulfill the decree ʿof torment˧ against the disbelievers.

Meaning, the Quran was revealed as a warning and reminder for those who are alive; those whose hearts are alive and are able to comprehend the message of the Quran. The word ḥayy here is referring to those whose spiritual hearts are alive giving them the ability to understand, comprehend, and process the truth. Another objective of the Quran is to establish proof against the non-believers. Once they have received revelation, they can no longer claim ignorance as an excuse. This verse is telling us that the Quran is a mercy for the believers and a proof and evidence against the non-believers. Syed Quṭb writes, "Here the Quranic expression contrasts disbelief with life, making unbelief equal to death and propensity to faith equal to life. Thus, the Quran has been revealed to the

Prophet Muḥammad ﷺ so as to warn those who are alive and can benefit from the warning. The non-believers, on the other hand, are dead and cannot hear the warning. Therefore, the function of the Quran, in as far as they are concerned, is to record their situation which makes them deserve punishment. God will not inflict punishment on anyone who has not received His message. Punishment is for those who did receive His message and who were determined to disbelieve in it, thereby writing their own ruin."[75]

Allah ﷻ now returns to the topic of His oneness and some of the irrefutable and magnificent signs and proofs of His absolute might, power, and magnificence.

أَوَلَمْ يَرَوْا أَنَّا خَلَقْنَا لَهُم مِّمَّا عَمِلَتْ أَيْدِينَآ أَنْعَـٰمًا فَهُمْ لَهَا مَـٰلِكُونَ ۝

[71] Do they not see that We single handedly created for them, among other things, cattle which are under their control?

Do the non-believers of Makkah and others not see with their own eyes that Allah ﷻ has created an'ām, which includes camels, cows and sheep, for them? "Do they not see?" is a rhetorical question referring to understanding and comprehension. Allah ﷻ wants them to use their intellect to recognize and acknowledge this immense blessing that they take for granted. Don't they realize, recognize, and understand that cattle - camels, cows, sheeps, and goats - were created by Allah ﷻ specifically for the benefit of mankind? This sign is something that they were very familiar

---

75   Quṭb, *fī Ẓilāl al-Quran*, 4:2975

with. They did not have to go look for it or explore in some far off land. The cattle were right in front of their eyes. Not only did Allah ﷻ create these animals for mankind's benefit, He also placed them under their control. These animals have been made subservient to humanity so that we can use them for our own benefit.

Allah ﷻ then describes some of the benefits derived from these animals in order to create a sense and feeling of gratitude within their hearts.

وَذَلَّلْنَـٰهَا لَهُـمْ فَمِنْهَا رَكُوبُهُـمْ وَمِنْهَا يَأْكُلُونَ ۝ وَلَهُمْ فِيهَا مَنَـٰفِعُ وَمَشَارِبُ أَفَـلَا يَشْكُرُونَ ۝

⁷² And We have subjected these ˹animals˺ to them, so they may ride some and eat others. ⁷³ And they derive from them other benefits and drinks. Will they not then give thanks?

For many of us, these blessings may not seem very immediate and tangible because we live in urban settings. We come from concrete jungles, where the grass has been replaced by asphalt, trees with street lamps, and mountains with buildings. We are disconnected from nature and the natural world. We are far removed from owning cattle; riding them, milking them, churning butter, making cheese or cream, slaughtering animals, tanning hides, producing leather, making clothes, and using the bones to make various tools and utensils. We live in an environment of mass production, industrialization, and factories. For the initial recipients of revelation who lived in the desert and for those who live in more rural settings, these verses are much more powerful and profound. They are being reminded about signs and blessings that are immediate, real, and tangible. Allah ﷻ is reminding the audience that He alone has subjected these animals under our control. A young child is able to tame and train a large and strong camel. These animals that are bigger and stronger than us, have been placed under our care and control. We are able to use some animals as a means of transportation and traveling and as a source of food and nutrition. We also use these animals for their milk and several other benefits. Almost every part of the body of a camel, cow, and sheep can be used by us.

We are reminded about these blessings throughout the Quran. Allah ﷻ says in Sūrah al-Naḥl, "And He created the cattle for you as a source of warmth, food, and ˹many other˺ benefits. They are also pleasing to you when you bring them home and when you take them out to graze. And they carry your loads to ˹distant˺ lands which you could not otherwise reach without great hardship. Surely your Lord is Ever Gracious, Most Merciful. ˹He also created˺ horses, mules, and donkeys for your transportation and adornment. And He creates what you do not know."[76] Later on, in the same Sūrah, Allah ﷻ reminds us, "And there is certainly a lesson for you in cattle: We give you to drink of what is in their bellies, from between digested food and blood: pure milk, pleasant to drink."[77]

After reminding us about all of these amazing favors, gifts, and blessings Allah ﷻ asks, "Will they not then give thanks?" After recognizing that all of these amazing gifts are from Allah ﷻ, will they not be grateful? Should they not be grateful to the One Who created all of this for them? Although this statement is posed as a question, it is really a direct order to be grateful to the Creator of all these amazing blessings through submission, devotion, obedience, servitude, and worship. Reflection upon Allah's blessings naturally leads towards a deep feeling of gratitude, thanks, and appreciation. Syed Quṭb remarks, "When we look at the matter in this Quranic light we are bound to feel that God's blessings overflow from every corner around us. Thus, every time we ride an animal, eat a piece of meat, have a drink of milk, taste a piece of cheese or use fat for cooking, or wear a garment made of

---

76   16:5-9 - وَالْأَنْعَامَ خَلَقَهَا ۗ لَكُمْ فِيهَا دِفْءٌ وَمَنَافِعُ وَمِنْهَا تَأْكُلُونَ * وَلَكُمْ فِيهَا جَمَالٌ حِينَ تُرِيحُونَ وَحِينَ تَسْرَحُونَ *وَتَحْمِلُ أَثْقَالَكُمْ إِلَى بَلَدٍ لَّمْ تَكُونُوا بَالِغِيهِ إِلَّا بِشِقِّ الْأَنفُسِ إِنَّ رَبَّكُمْ لَرَءُوفٌ رَّحِيمٌ * وَالْخَيْلَ وَالْبِغَالَ وَالْحَمِيرَ لِتَرْكَبُوهَا وَزِينَةً ۚ وَيَخْلُقُ مَا لَا تَعْلَمُونَ

77   16:66 - وَإِنَّ لَكُمْ فِي الْأَنْعَامِ لَعِبْرَةً ۖ نُّسْقِيكُم مِّمَّا فِي بُطُونِهِ مِن بَيْنِ فَرْثٍ وَدَمٍ لَّبَنًا خَالِصًا سَائِغًا لِّلشَّارِبِينَ

hide, wool or animal hair, we, in our hearts, feel God's endless blessings and infinite grace. This, then, applies to all things around us and everything we use, whether animate or inanimate. All our lives, then, become a continuous act of glorifying God and giving thanks to Him."[78]

However, the non-believers - in this context the pagans of Arabia, but it also includes atheists, agnostics, and anyone who refuses to accept the truth - fail to recognize the Power and Being behind everything they see and feel around them. They refuse to recognize the blessings of Allah and remain persistent in their denial and rejection of the truth. So much so that they leave worshiping the Creator and turn towards the worship of things that can neither give benefit or harm. They even have false hopes and expectations of help from them.

وَٱتَّخَذُوا مِن دُونِ ٱللَّهِ ءَالِهَةً لَّعَلَّهُمْ يُنصَرُونَ ۝ لَا يَسْتَطِيعُونَ نَصْرَهُمْ وَهُمْ لَهُمْ جُندٌ مُّحْضَرُونَ ۝

[74] Still they have taken other gods besides Allah, hoping to be helped (by them). [75] They cannot help the pagans, even though they serve the idols as dedicated guards.

The pagans and those who follow in their footsteps "have taken other gods besides Allah." They have adopted material objects, created things, and ideas as gods worthy of worship besides Allah. The pagans during the time of the Prophet worshiped idols and statues, inanimate objects, that they created and shaped with their own hands. In the

---

78   Quṭb, *fī Ẓilāl al-Quran*, 5:2976

modern era, in addition to worshiping idols and statues, people have adopted figurative idols as objects worthy of worship and devotion such as wealth, the self, desires, and certain ideologies. They have taken other gods besides Allah ﷻ "hoping to be helped (by them)." The pagans place false hopes in them; hoping that these idols and statues will help them, provide for them, take care of them, benefit them, and protect them from harm in this world and the next.

However, in reality, they cannot do anything whatsoever. They are useless inanimate objects that cannot help themselves let alone anyone or anything else. "They cannot help the pagans, even though they serve the idols as dedicated guards." The idols and statues - the false gods - cannot help them in any way, shape, or form. The pagans "serve the idols as dedicated guards" by worshiping them and defending them from verbal and physical attacks. The pagans would worship and serve the idols with false hopes of getting closer to Allah ﷻ and earning safety and protection in this world and the next. Allah ﷻ mentions this to highlight the absurdity of worshiping idols and taking other gods besides Allah ﷻ. How can you worship an inanimate object expecting it to benefit you, when it cannot even protect itself? How can you worship something that you created with your own two hands that does not speak, hear, cause benefit, or prevent harm?

Allah ﷻ then consoles, comforts, and reassures the Prophet ﷺ reminding him to remain patient, firm, strong, and steadfast.

فَلَا يَحْزُنكَ قَوْلُهُمْ إِنَّا نَعْلَمُ مَا يُسِرُّونَ وَمَا يُعْلِنُونَ ۝

⁷⁶ So do not let their words grieve you [O Prophet]. Indeed,
We [fully] know what they conceal and what they reveal.

Allah ﷻ is comforting, consoling, and reassuring the Prophet ﷺ; do not be so sad, distraught, and depressed at their refusal to believe in the Quran. Do not grieve out of sorrow for them if they refuse to accept the message. Do not let their harsh words, false accusations, and outlandish claims grieve you. Your responsibility is simply to convey the message; you are not responsible for what they do with it. Once they have received the message they are responsible for their own decisions. If they accept the truth, then they will be benefiting themselves, and if they reject it, then they will only be harming themselves. "Indeed, We [fully] know what they conceal and what they reveal." Allah ﷻ is reminding the Prophet ﷺ that He is fully aware of what they are saying and doing, and will hold them accountable, if not in this world, then the next.

In the next few verses, Allah ﷻ once again returns to the topic of the Day of Resurrection. He ﷻ mentions a doubt of those who disbelieve and answers their doubt with three answers. It is narrated that once Ubay ibn Khalaf came to the Prophet ﷺ with an old brittle bone and crumbled it in his hand. He then said, "O Muḥammad! Will Allah resurrect this after it has turned to dust?" The Prophet ﷺ replied, "Yes, Allah will resurrect this. And he will cause you to die and bring you back to life, and He will enter you into the fire of hell." The following verses were then revealed.

أَوَلَمْ يَرَ ٱلْإِنسَـٰنُ أَنَّا خَلَقْنَـٰهُ مِن نُّطْفَةٍ فَإِذَا هُوَ خَصِيمٌ مُّبِينٌ ۝ وَضَرَبَ لَنَا مَثَلًا وَنَسِيَ خَلْقَهُۥ قَالَ مَن يُحْىِ ٱلْعِظَـٰمَ وَهِىَ رَمِيمٌ ۝ قُلْ يُحْيِيهَا ٱلَّذِىٓ أَنشَأَهَآ أَوَّلَ مَرَّةٍ وَهُوَ بِكُلِّ خَلْقٍ عَلِيمٌ ۝ ٱلَّذِى جَعَلَ لَكُم مِّنَ ٱلشَّجَرِ ٱلْأَخْضَرِ نَارًا فَإِذَآ أَنتُم

مِّنْـهُ تُوقِـدُونَ ۝

⁷⁷ Do people not see that We have created them from a sperm-drop, then—behold!—they openly challenge [Us]? ⁷⁸ And they argue with Us—forgetting they were created—saying, "Who will give life to decayed bones?" ⁷⁹ Say, [O Prophet,] "They will be revived by the One Who produced them the first time, for He has [perfect] knowledge of every created being. ⁸⁰ [He is the One] Who gives you fire from green trees, and—behold!—you kindle [fire] from them.

Allah ﷻ opens these few verses by asking rhetorically, "Do people not see that We have created them from a sperm-drop?" Does everyone not know that I created them from a weak impure substance - a drop of sperm - and then gradually shaped and formed them into a complete human being? This is an observable reality of life that no human can deny. "Then—behold!—they openly challenge [Us]." Now, all of a sudden, this weak, frail, dependent, and incapable human thinks they are strong, independent, and intelligent, so they argue against Me and My ability to bring the dead back to life. They challenge my infinite might, power, glory, and magnificence. One of the purposes of this rhetorical question is to cause those who refuse to believe in resurrection to ponder over their own creation, which should lead them to the conclusion that indeed, Allah ﷻ is able to bring the dead back to life. If anything, it is is easier than their original creation.

"And they argue with Us—forgetting they were created—saying, 'Who will give life to decayed bones?'" The challenge to Allah's infinite might and power is absolutely ridiculous and asinine. This ungrateful human asks how life can be given to bones after they decay, decompose, and turn to dust? Does this human not remember how they were created from something weaker? They have forgotten their origin; that they were created from an insignificant drop of sperm. Allah ﷻ Himself instructs the Prophet ﷺ on how to answer their doubt.

"Say, [O Prophet,] 'They will be revived by the One Who produced them the first time, for He has [perfect] knowledge of every created being. [He is the One] Who gives you fire from green trees, and—behold!—you kindle [fire] from them.'" Allah ﷻ is addressing the Prophet ﷺ and telling him to respond to Ubayy and anyone else who doubts the reality of life after death that these bones that have decayed and turned to dust will be brought back to life by the same Being Who created them the first time. They will be brought back to life by Allah ﷻ, the Originator, Who created and brought everything into existence from nothing. He ﷻ has perfect knowledge of all things, which includes His knowledge of initial creation and resurrection.

The Prophet ﷺ is told to describe Allah ﷻ as the One "Who gives you fire from green trees, and—behold!—you kindle [fire] from them." This is to make those who reject life after death realize that not only is it a possibility, it is an absolute reality. They witness Allah's might and power when they kindle fire from fresh green trees. Humans, through exploration and experimentation, were able to discover the ability to kindle fire by rubbing twigs of a tree together. These green trees full of water and liquid are able to produce fire through friction. Just as Allah ﷻ is able to make fire emerge from wood that is moist and wet, He ﷻ is also able to cause life to emerge from bones that are dead and decayed.

أَوَلَيْسَ ٱلَّذِى خَلَقَ ٱلسَّمَٰوَٰتِ وَٱلْأَرْضَ بِقَٰدِرٍ عَلَىٰ أَن يَخْلُقَ مِثْلَهُم بَلَىٰ وَهُوَ ٱلْخَلَّٰقُ ٱلْعَلِيمُ ۞

⁸¹ Is He Who created the heavens and earth not able to create the likes of these people? Of course He is! He is the All Knowing Master Creator:

This is a rhetorical question posed by Allah ﷻ to those who refused to believe in life after death. The purpose of this question is to make them realize the infinite might and power of Allah ﷻ; to engage their intellect and lead them to the rational conclusion that the One Who created the heavens and the earth is definitely able to bring the dead back to life. Although this is posed as a rhetorical question, the meaning conveyed by it is that of a factual statement. The One Who created the heavens and everything they contain - the billions of galaxies, the sun, moon, stars, planets, and other celestial bodies - and the One Who created the Earth and everything it contains - the mountains, valleys, plains, rivers, oceans, lakes, trees, and anything we can think of - is definitely able to create the likes of these people. There is absolutely no doubt about it whatsoever. "Of course He is!" Of course Allah ﷻ is able to create anything He wills according to His divine knowledge and wisdom. He is al-Khallāq, the Master Creator, the One Who designed, fashioned, originated, and created everything that exists. He is al-ʿAlīm, the All-Knowing, Whose knowledge is infinite, limitless, and ecompasses every single thing.

This same idea and concept is echoed throughout the Quran. For example, Allah ﷻ says in Sūrah Ghāfir, "The creation of the heavens and the earth is certainly greater than the re-creation of humankind, but most people do not know."[79] Similarly, Allah ﷻ says in Sūrah al-Aḥqāf, "Do they not realize that Allah, Who created the heavens and the earth and did not tire in creating them, is able to give life to the dead? Yes [indeed]! He is certainly Most Capable of everything."[80]

---

79   40:57 - لَخَلْقُ السَّمَاوَاتِ وَالْأَرْضِ أَكْبَرُ مِنْ خَلْقِ النَّاسِ وَلَكِنَّ أَكْثَرَ النَّاسِ لَا يَعْلَمُونَ

80   46:33 - أَوَلَمْ يَرَوْا أَنَّ اللَّه الَّذِى خَلَقَ السَّمَاوَاتِ وَالْأَرْضَ وَلَمْ يَعْيَ بِخَلْقِهِنَّ بِقَادِرٍ عَلَى أَن يُحْيِيَ الْمَوْتَى بَلَى إِنَّهُ عَلَى كُلِّ شَىْءٍ قَدِيرٌ

إِنَّمَآ أَمْرُهُۥٓ إِذَآ أَرَادَ شَيْئًا أَن يَقُولَ لَهُۥ كُن فَيَكُونُ ۝

82 All it takes, when He wills something ˹to be˺, is simply
to say to it: "Be!" And it is!

Allah ﷻ is the Almighty the All-Powerful. His might and power is beyond human imagination. When He wants something to be, not happen, come into existence, or anything of the sort, He simply says, "Be!" and it is. This entire universe and everything it contains is a manifestation of the infinite might and power of Allah ﷻ.

فَسُبْحَـٰنَ ٱلَّذِى بِيَدِهِۦ مَلَكُوتُ كُلِّ شَىْءٍ وَإِلَيْهِ تُرْجَعُونَ ۝

83 So glory be to the One in Whose Hands is the authority over all things, and to Whom ˹alone˺ you will ˹all˺ be returned.

This is a declaration of the absolute perfection of Allah ﷻ. Subḥān, glory be, signifies that Allah ﷻ is far above and beyond anything the pagans associate with Him. It also conveys amazement and shock at their absurd claims. Allah ﷻ alone is the absolute owner, king, ruler, controller, and Lord of everything that exists in this universe; He ﷻ is the King of all kings. Allah ﷻ concludes this very beautiful and powerful Sūrah by reminding us about our final destination, "to Whom (alone) you will (all) be returned." Every single human being, from the beginning of time until the end of time, every single one of us, will be returned to our Lord and Creator.

That brings us to the end of this very powerful, profound, eloquent, and beautiful chapter of the Quran that is meant to penetrate the depths of our hearts, moving them and shaking them, into true submission of the Divine. The main themes and concepts of this Sūrah revolve around the fundamentals of faith and belief; belief in Allah ﷻ, His Messenger ﷺ, and the Last Day. Reciting this Sūrah with understanding and reflection is a means of fortifying our faith, getting closer to Allah ﷻ, and nurturing and developing a true mindset of God-consciousness. The purpose behind our recitation and study of the Quran is to engage in deep reflection and extract practical lessons, morals, and guidance. May Allah ﷻ grant all of us the ability to recite the Quran, understand its message, and implement its guidance into our daily lives.

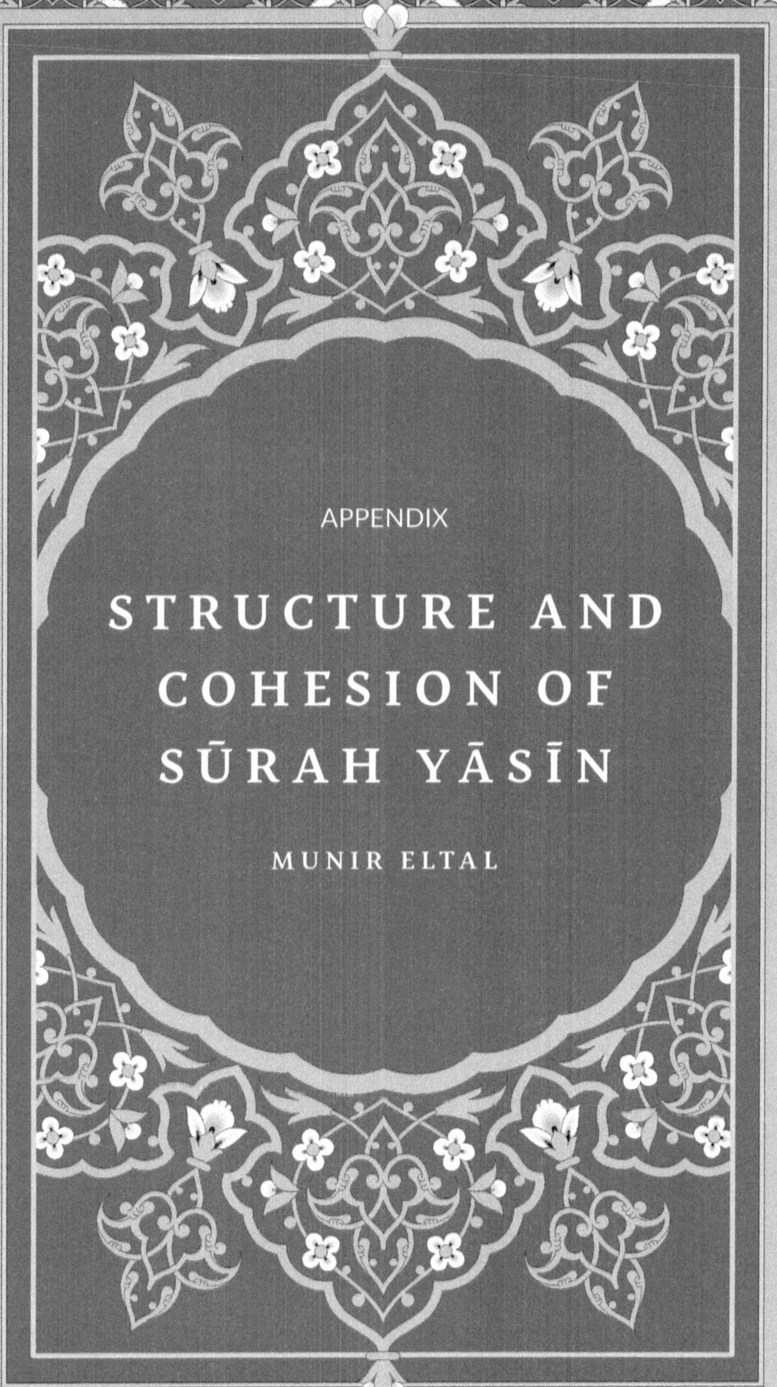

APPENDIX

STRUCTURE AND COHESION OF SŪRAH YĀSĪN

MUNIR ELTAL

In the Name of Allah, the Most Merciful, the Very Merciful. All thanks and praise are due to Allah ﷻ, the Master of all creation, and may His blessings be upon His last and final Messenger, Muḥammad ﷺ, his family, his companions, and those who follow them until the end of times.

A cursory glance at *tafsīr (scholarly interpretation)* works is enough to appreciate the rich meaning embedded in every letter of the Quran. As Furhan Zubairi demonstrated prior, the lessons are endless, and the application of those wisdoms is a lifelong journey. But an often-overlooked aspect of the Quran is its organization. How do the *āyāt* come together to form a coherent whole whose placement of *āyāt* contributes to a well-organized and methodological message and *sūrah*? And how might that structuring lend itself to uncovering deeper meanings not as apparent on an initial read through?

I am not simply referring to how context plays a pivotal role in properly understanding any given *āyah* in the Quran, as that has been well-documented. I am speaking more broadly about how the overall *sūrah* is composed. Just as one can take a book and understand its full outline – typically linear with Chapter 1 leading to Chapter 2, Chapter 2 to Chapter 3, etc. – surely the Quran has its own outline that we can observe and understand.

However, before one answers the aforementioned questions, it is important to ask why studying *naẓm*[1] *(composition)* is meaningful in the first place. Why should one study how Allah ﷻ organized the placement of His *āyāt*? There are five reasons worth discussing:

1.

Allah ﷻ is the Best of Speakers and His Speech is the Best of All Speech - Allah ﷻ says in the beginning of *Sūrah al-Raḥmān (The Most Merciful)*, "The Most Merciful, He taught the Quran, created man, [and] taught him *al-bayān*."[2] *Bayān* involves both expressing oneself and understanding what has been expressed by others. It can be defined as eloquence, clear speech, explaining, the ability to express oneself, or elucidating.

Allah ﷻ taught humans how to speak, and part of communicating effectively is having organized speech. If all of coherent speech is clearly organized, what can be said of the speech of the teacher of all speech? Part of the agreed upon definition of the Quran is that it is the **inimitable** speech of Allah ﷻ. Nothing can, or will, ever come close to His words in all praiseworthy manners. Allah ﷻ Himself calls the Quran *"bayān,"* so one should take note of how He organized His perfect words.

Additionally, in *Sūrah al-Kahf (The Cave)* Allah ﷻ says, "Say, 'If the sea were ink for [writing] the words of my Lord, the sea would be exhausted before the words of my Lord were exhausted, even if We brought the like of it as a supplement.'"[3] And He ﷻ also says in *Sūrah Luqmān (Luqmān the Wise)*, "And if whatever trees upon the earth were pens and the sea [was ink], replenished thereafter by seven [more] seas, the words of Allah would not be exhausted. Indeed, Allah is Exalted in Might and Wise."[4] These *āyāt* point to Allah's ability to articulate meanings with many layers of understanding.

---

1 Randhawa and Khan succinctly summarize the meaning of naẓm in their book, <u>Divine Speech: Exploring the Quran as Literature</u>, as "'arrangement,' 'order,' or 'organization.' It signifies the arrangement of individual parts into a coherent whole. For example, this word is used for stringing beads or pearls together to produce a beautiful necklace, or the arrangement of a set of wells into a uniform layout. It is also used to refer to the 'contiguity' of a series of items, or how a group of items 'stick' or 'cohere' together."

2 الرَّحْمَـٰنُ * عَلَّمَ الْقُرْآنَ * خَلَقَ الْإِنسَانَ * عَلَّمَهُ الْبَيَانَ - 55:1-4

3 قُل لَّوْ كَانَ الْبَحْـرُ مِـدَادًا لِّكَلِمَـاتِ رَبِّي لَنَفِـدَ الْبَحْـرُ قَبْـلَ أَن تَنفَـدَ كَلِمَـاتُ رَبِّي وَلَوْ - 18:109 جِئْنَـا بِمِثْلِـهِ مَـدَدًا

4 وَلَوْ أَنَّمَـا فِي الْأَرْضِ مِـن شَـجَرَةٍ أَقْـلَامٌ وَالْبَحْـرُ يَمُـدُّهُ مِـن بَعْـدِهِ سَـبْعَةُ أَبْحُـرٍ مَّـا - 31:27 نَفِـدَتْ كَلِمَـاتُ اللَّـهِ إِنَّ اللَّـهَ عَزِيـزٌ حَكِيـمٌ

The more one delves into His *āyāt*, the more one benefits and finds. How He structured His words may be another layer on top of the already innumerable methods of accessing Allah's message.

2.

All of Creation is Organized[5] – Humans are encouraged by Allah ﷻ in a number of āyāt to contemplate the harmony of His creation. In *Sūrah al-Wāqiʿah (The Inevitable)*, Allah ﷻ says, "I swear by the positions of the stars—A mighty oath, if you only knew—that this is truly a noble Quran."[6] Allah ﷻ tied the precision of the star's positions to the Quran. If the heavens, the earth, the cells in our bodies and even the atoms forming those objects are organized, then how can the speech of Allah ﷻ not be?

Science and mathematics are essentially the study of how Allah ﷻ organized His creation. If not for the regular patterns one witnesses in the world, documenting observations into comprehensible textbooks and research papers would be near-impossible. Just as creation has a structure one can follow, the structure of Allah's speech is also observable.

3.

There Are Claims That the Quran is Unorganized - There are many documented cases of non-Muslims critiquing the Quran for what they perceive to be a lack of cohesion. The French philosopher, Voltaire, wrote scathingly about Islam. On the Quran in particular, he is recorded to have stated, "The Qur'an is a rhapsody without liaison, without order, without art; it is said nevertheless that this boring book is a very beautiful book—I am referring here to the Arabs, who pretend it is written with an elegance and a purity that no one has approached since."[7]

There are also those such as Thomas Carlyle who generally spoke favorably about Islam. He said in praise of the Messenger ﷺ, "It is a great shame for anyone to listen to the accusation that Islam is a lie and that Muhammad was a fabricator and a deceiver. We saw that he remained steadfast upon

---

5   This point is argued in more detail by Shaykh Hamīduddīn Farāhī in his book, *Dalāil an-Niẓām*

6   فَلَا أُقْسِمُ بِمَوَاقِعِ النُّجُومِ * وَإِنَّهُ لَقَسَمٌ لَّوْ تَعْلَمُونَ عَظِيمٌ * إِنَّهُ لَقُرْآنٌ كَرِيمٌ - 56:75

7   Voltaire, "Alcoran" in *Dictionnaire de philosophie*, cited in Michel Cuypers and Geneviève Gobillot, *Le Coran* (Paris: Le Cavalier Bleu, 2007)

his principles, with firm determination; kind and generous, compassionate, pious, virtuous, with real manhood, hardworking and sincere. Besides all these qualities, he was lenient with others, tolerant, kind, cheerful and praiseworthy and perhaps he would joke and tease his companions. He was just, truthful, smart, pure, magnanimous and present-minded; his face was radiant as if he had lights within him to illuminate the darkest of nights; he was a great man by nature who was not educated in a school nor nurtured by a teacher as he was not in need of any of this."[8] Which makes his criticism of the Quran all the more impactful when he said, "I must say, it is as toilsome reading as I ever undertook. A wearisome confused jumble, crude, incondite; endless iterations, long-windedness, entanglement [...] insupportable stupidity in short!"[9]

Then there are the Muslims, though sincere in their questioning, who are confused about how Allah ﷻ organized His speech. What many fail to realize is that the Quran has its own standard of structure, one which is better than anything on offer from Allah's creation. Despite the lofty standards, Allah ﷻ tells us in the beginning of *Sūrah Yūsuf (Joseph)*, "No doubt We sent it down as an Arabic Quran so that you all may understand [it]."[10] The coherence of the Quran is accessible, and this book will demonstrate, at a surface level, how well-structured a *sūrah* can be.

4.

The Arrangement of the Quran is Not Chronological — While there are differences of opinion on who ultimately decided on the current order of the *suwar* in the written copy of the Quran we have today,[11] there is no doubt that the **suwar** are **not** in the chronological order that they were revealed in. If we assume Allah ﷻ to be the organizer of the Quran, then this points to there being a wisdom in their current order that would have been lost had the original chronology been preserved. In other words, Allah ﷻ intended for the Quran to be rearranged and compiled into its current order for us to

---

8 Carlyle, *Thomas Carlyle, On Heroes, Hero Worship and the Heroic in History*, ed. Archibald MacMechan (Boston: Athenaeum, 1901)

9 Ibid.

10 إِنَّا أَنزَلْنَاهُ قُرْآنًا عَرَبِيًّا لَّعَلَّكُمْ تَعْقِلُونَ - 12:2

11 As I will argue in this book, I believe the current order to be divinely inspired by Allah ﷻ.

study and benefit from.

On that note, it is possible that Western scholars' frustration with the existing arrangement of suwar is what spurred on their attempts to reconstruct the chronological order of the Quran.[12]

5.

It is a Potential Source for Interpreting the Quran - *Tafsīr* of the Quran with the Quran is one of the main sources for unlocking the Quran's meanings. Imām as-Suyūṭī summarized this methodology saying, "The scholars have said: Whoever wishes to interpret the Quran, he should first turn to the Quran itself. This is because what has been narrated briefly in one place might be explained in detail in another place, and what is summarized in one place might be explained in another."[13] In simpler terms, using the surrounding context can help to elucidate the meaning of Allah's words. By understanding how Allah ﷻ organized the *āyāt*, qualified scholars may be able to uncover an additional layer of context by which to interpret a *sūrah*.

Part of understanding the Quran is in asking questions, thus observing how and why Allah ﷻ structured His Word opens the doors to new questions and potentially new insights.

ORGANIZING TOOLS

Before beginning the breakdown of the structure of *Sūrah YāSīn*, it is important to understand the different methods of organizing communication. The study of the composition of a sūrah involves several aspects. It has been observed that Allah ﷻ utilizes the following tools to varying degrees, with each providing a unique benefit.

LINEAR COHERENCE

The most familiar type of organization to Western audiences is called **linear coherence**, which concerns the linear flow, continuity or sequential arrangement of the Quran. In what way is one *āyah* or topic connected to the next? This is how any modern text (including this book) is written. Idea #1

---

12   Mir, Mustansir. "Coherence in the Quran," 1986.

13   as-Suyūṭī, *Al-Itqān fī 'ulūm al-Qurān*

leads to Idea #2, which leads to Idea #3, etc. Linear coherence has the most written about it with regards to the Quran, and as such, there will not be too much focus on this method during our studies. [14]

PARALLELISM

There are two main types of symmetrical patterns. The first we will explore is called Parallelism. This is when parts of a composition are ordered on the pattern of ABC/A'B'C'. Rāzī demonstrated this in his observations between *Sūra Mā'ūn* and *Sūrah al-Kawthar*. By way of another example, Allah ﷻ says in *Sūrah Qāf (Qāf)* (transliteration provided where needed)[15]:

A - But they **denied** *(kadhdhabū)*
B - **the truth** *(al-Ḥaqq)* when it came to them,
C - so they are in a **confused** *(marīj)* condition. (5)
D - Have they not looked at the heaven above them - **how We structured it** and **adorned it** and [how] it has no rifts? (6) And the earth - **We spread it out** and **cast therein** firmly set mountains and **made grow** therein [something] of every beautiful kind, (7) Giving insight and a reminder for every servant who turns [to Allah]. (8) And We have sent down blessed rain from the sky and **made grow** thereby gardens and grain from the harvest (9) And lofty palm trees having fruit arranged in layers - (10) As provision for the servants, and We have **given life thereby to a dead land. Thus is the resurrection.** (11)
A' - The people of Noah **denied** *(khadhdhabat)* before them, and the companions of the well and Thamud (12) And 'Aad and Pharaoh and the brothers of Lot (13) And the companions of the thicket and the people of Tubba'. All **denied** *(khadhdhaba)* the messengers,
B' - so My threat was **truly** *(ḥaqqa)* fulfilled. (14)

---

14   The interested reader may read the aforementioned, *"an-Naẓm ad-Durar fi tanāsub al-āyāt wa as-Suwar (The Arrangement of Pearls with Regards to the Connections of the Āyāt and Suwar)"* by al-Baqā'ī.

15   Heavenly Order. *"Sūrah Qāf* (Part 2)." 2 Oct. 2020, https://heavenlyorder.substack.com/p/surah-qaaf-part-2.

> **C'** - Did We fail in the first creation? But they are in **confusion** (*labsin*)
>
> **D'** - over a **new creation** (15)

Each item corresponds to its source in the list. The point is that the parallel terms must have some conspicuous relationship, whether it is a relationship of similarity, opposites, or something else.

Parallelism is an extremely common device in poetics and rhetoric, because it is simple, intuitive, aesthetically appealing, and poetically moving.[16] In terms of the Quran, if one finds a parallel pattern, then Allah ﷻ could be drawing attention to an otherwise overlooked relationship between two items. Conversely, where all but one item corresponds in a parallel structure, it may be that Allah ﷻ is teaching us a lesson about the subtle differences.

MIRROR COMPOSITION

The second type of symmetrical form may be called inverted parallelism, concentric, or **mirror composition**. This is where the terms or ideas are presented in one order but then repeated in the reverse order. This follows the pattern ABC/C'B'A'. In a similar vein, the term **ring composition** is used to describe such a structure when it contains a discrete center. It could either have a stand-alone centerpiece that connects the two halves (as in ABCB'A') or simply be a mirror composition on a large or complex scale, such as ABC-D/D'C'B'A', in which D/D' might be considered the center. This structure was mentioned for *Āyah al-Kursī*, above. As another example, the story of Mūsā in *Sūrat al-Qaṣaṣ (The Story)* also appears to be structured in this manner[17]:

> **A** – Prologue (1-6)
>
> **B** – Moses is thrown in the water and lives (7-8)
>
> **C** – The Pharaoh's wife asks him for a favor (9)
>
> **D** – The sister of Moses is sent to Pharaoh and her speech is accepted (10-12)

---

16   Ali Khan, Nouman and Sharif Randhawa. Divine Speech: *Exploring the Quran as Literature.* Bayyinah Institute, 2016.

17   Heavenly Order. "Sūrah Al-Qaṣaṣ (Part 1)." 6 Nov. 2020, heavenlyorder.substack.com/p/surah-al-qaa-part-1.

<table>
<tr><td colspan="3">E – Moses is returned to his mother (13)</td></tr>
<tr><td></td><td colspan="2">F – Moses unsuccessfully tries to help a man twice (14-22)</td></tr>
<tr><td></td><td colspan="2">F' – Moses successfully helps two women on the first try (23-24)</td></tr>
<tr><td colspan="3">E' – Moses meets his father-in-law (25-28)</td></tr>
<tr><td colspan="3">D' – Moses is sent to Pharaoh and his speech is rejected (29-37)</td></tr>
<tr><td colspan="3">C' – Pharaoh asks Haman for a favor (38)</td></tr>
<tr><td colspan="3">B' – Pharaoh and his army voluntarily enter the sea and are drowned (39-42)</td></tr>
<tr><td colspan="3">A' – Epilogue (43-52)</td></tr>
</table>

Several features are significant about ring composition. First, it may occur on different scales. It can be seen in sentences, passages, or even an entire book. In some cases, as is common in the Quran, a large-scale ring composition consists, in turn, of smaller rings.

Finally, understanding ring structure can be important for understanding the meaning of a composition. In a ring composition, usually "the meaning is located in the middle;"[18] that is, the center of the composition literally underscores the central idea. The two halves of the composition may be seen as elaborations of that theme, and the beginning and the ending segments (A and A') introduce and conclude that theme. Moreover, the ring structure points to common themes that underlie the two corresponding terms or segments on the opposite sides of the structure. In essence the ring manifests the relationship between the parts and reveals the logic of the composition. It is important to add that the relationship between the two corresponding segments (e.g., B and B') does not always have to be immediately obvious. The discovery of a ring structure forces the audience to contemplate and uncover the relationship between the corresponding parts. [19]

INTEGRATIVE COHERENCE

The fourth aspect of coherence to explore is called the **integrative co-**

---

18 See Mary Douglas, Thinking in Circles: An Essay on Ring Composition (New Haven/London: Yale University Press, 2007)

19 Ibid.

herence of a *sūrah*. This is concerned with how different *āyāt*, passages, or sections within a sūrah, or even between separate *suwar*, are interconnected by key terms, verbal roots, images, parallel expressions, or even sound patterns that they share. To simplify, we will call these unifying items **anchors**.

Although this sort of study is already known more formally as intertextuality, we will use the term "integrative coherence" to emphasize the role of these anchors in:

- Integrating different parts of a section together
- Linking separate sections of a sūrah, thereby helping to unify it
- Linking āyāt or passages from separate suwar[20]

HOLISTIC COHERENCE

Finally, each of these approaches contributes to understanding the *sūrah's* **holistic coherence**; how the *sūrah* is united into a consistent and distinct whole. In this regard, one might be interested in identifying a **motif**, an overarching idea that unites and explains all of the sūrah's contents or components. In addition to seeing the unity of an individual sūrah and how each part of it fits into the scheme of the whole, one might also be interested in understanding the role of the *sūrah* in a broader *sūrah* pair or group, or in the Quran as a whole. [21]

The study of holistic coherence is a method of the reader inquiring, "Why is this *āyah* placed in **this** sūrah and not another one?" The immediate context creates a meaning that may be altered if the *āyah* were placed elsewhere in the Quran.

FINAL NOTES

Before continuing, it is important to emphasize that the organizing structures mentioned above are not unique to the Quran. They have been used in other ancient texts across cultures. For example, ring composition was extremely widespread in the ancient world, and even up until modern times. As noted by Randhawa and Khan, "After its discovery in the Hebrew Bible, scholars in other fields of literature have uncovered ring composition

---

20   Ali Khan, Nouman and Sharif Randhawa. Divine Speech: Exploring the Quran as Literature. Bayyinah Institute, 2016.

21   Ibid.

in such diverse works as Homer's *Iliad* in Greek; the Gathas, hyms attributed to the Iranian prophet Zoroaster in the Avestan language; Classical Arabic poetry; Chinese literature; the medieval Persian *Mathnawi* of Rumi; medieval European epic poems such as the Old English *Beowulf*, the French epic poem chanson de geste, and medieval German *Nibelungenlied*; modern English poems such as John Milton's *Paradise Lost* and Ezra Pound's *Cantos*; and various genres of oral recital in different parts of the world." [22, 23]

It is important to state that multiple organizational tools may be used to explore a single *sūrah*, and each tool may yield meanings different, but not contrary, to the others. As we will observe, the same passage may contain multiple structures layered on top of one-another. It is my belief that every *sūrah* of the Quran contains some overarching structure, organization, or cohesion that can be explored and observed, though my research is hitherto incomplete.

How I split up the passages and *āyāt* may also seem strange at first, as not every structure is split perfectly at the end of a *āyah*.[24] It is possible that one structure ends halfway through a *āyah* and another begins at the second half. It may also be the case that one section references a short phrase, while the corresponding section is an entire paragraph. These choices will all be justified below, but consider that Allah's standards for organizing His words may not match with what we consider "normal" from our limited experiences. What is explained briefly in one part may be expounded in a linked set of *āyāt* elsewhere.

Please keep in mind that the outlined observations below are just that; observations. I make no claims as to having presented **the** structure of a given *āyah* or section, let alone the entire *sūrah*. It is very possible that others will disagree with my proposed demarcations and that there are arguably better ways of splitting the *suwar* up. This is not meant to be an exhaustive

---

22   Ali Khan, Nouman and Sharif Randhawa. Divine Speech: Exploring the Quran as Literature. Bayyinah Institute, 2016.

23   See also Mary Douglas, Thinking in Circles: An Essay on Ring Composition (New Haven/London: Yale University Press, 2007), 4-12 and Raymond Farrin, Abundance from the Desert: Classical Arabic Poetry (Syracuse, NY: Syracuse University Press), 2011, xvii.

24   This does not take into consideration the differences of opinion on the number of *āyāt* in the Quran. For the uninitiated, I am not saying that there is a difference of opinion on the content of the Quran. This is a note about where different scholars opined some *āyāt* ended and began, resulting in a different number (but not content) of *āyāt* in a *sūrah*.

study of any *surah's* structure.

I have also tried my best to avoid making conclusions about the text based on a presented structure. In other words, this is **not** meant to be a *tafsīr* of the Quran's meanings. The hope is that qualified scholars take this work and use it appropriately.

With the above terminology understood, we may now begin the structural study *Sūrah YāSīn*. I will be omitting most Arabic from the forthcoming analysis and providing transliterations only when needed to draw a connection. Consult the Arabic[25] for the original wording of the Quran for any *āyāt* referenced below.

ORGANIZATION AND STRUCTURE OF *SŪRAH YĀSĪN*

Sūrah YāSīn (YāSīn) is the 36th *surah* of the Quran and is characterized by short *āyāt* and a fast rhythm making it easy to recite and memorize. It is a Meccan *surah*, with some commentators mentioning that it is the 41st *surah* to be revealed.

Similar to other Meccan revelation, *YāSīn* also discusses the three most fundamental aspects of our faith. It discusses *tawḥīd (oneness of Allah* ﷻ*)*, *risālah (prophethood and messengership)*, and *qiyāmah (resurrection and life after death)*. Out of these three fundamental themes, the most emphasis is given to the concept of resurrection.

Sūrah YāSīn (YāSīn)[26] can be divided into six passages or distinct subject matter. We will begin our discussion by looking at the connection within each passage individually, then we will return and observe the connection between all passages as a whole.

Quran And Our Record - Ring Structure Of *Āyāt* 1-12[27]

---

25   See Quran.com for the full translations of all the *suwar* we will study. If one has not already memorized the given *sūrah* under discussion, then even a single read-through of translation, before reading about its structure, will greatly help one understand the connections being proposed.

26   The following is based on the work of:
Ali Khan, Nouman. "Heavenly Order - Lesson 17_ Structural Coherence of Surah Ya-Sin" Bayyinah TV, https://bayyinahtv.com/topics/1/categories/1/series/28/videos/551

27   Khan's work on this particular section is built off of the observations made by Neal Robinson in <u>Discovering the Qur'an</u> (London: SCM Press Ltd, 1996), pages 151-152

A - YāSīn. (1) I swear by the Quran, rich in wisdom! (2) You are truly one of the messengers, (3) On a straight path. (4) [This is] a revelation of the Almighty, the Most Merciful, (5)

B - so that you may warn a people whose forefathers were not warned, and hence, they are unaware (6)

C - The decree has already been justified against most of them, for they do not believe. (7)

D - We have placed iron collars on their necks, so they are reaching up to their chins, and their heads are forced to remain upwards. (8) And We have placed a barrier in front of them and a barrier behind them, and (thus) they are covered by Us; so, they do not see. (9)

C' - It is the same whether you warn them or not—they will not believe. (10)

B' - You can only warn those who follow the Reminder and are in awe of the Most Compassionate without seeing Him. So, give them good news of forgiveness and an honorable reward. (11)

A' - Surely, We will give new life to the dead, and We are recording whatever (deeds) they send before them and whatever effects they leave behind. Everything is fully computed by Us in a perfect book of record. (12)

CONNECTIONS

[A]/[A'] - This section highlights two contrasting, but otherworldly, documents. The first is the Quran which is a document that was sent down from the heavens to the earth. The second is our book of deeds which are written on earth and then presented to Allah ﷻ above the seven heavens

[B]/[B'] - These passages share meaning as well as wording. Both use "*tundhir (you warn)*" to address the Messenger ﷺ. First, the Messenger ﷺ is told that he received revelation in order to warn people, and later he is told that only those who are fearful of Allah ﷻ can be warned.

[C]/[C'] - Here we find another shared phrase. Both parts say "*lā yu'minūn (they do not believe)*" in reference to the disbelievers. At first, we are told that they simply do not believe, but by the conclusion we learn that despite the warnings, they will never believe.

[D] - The center informs us of the consequences of their stubbornness to believe even when the truth has been made clear.

It is important to note that in the Quran, Allah ﷻ highlights three avenues for guidance:

1. From the **front** – by reflecting on the physical world in front of us
2. From the **back** – by reflecting on history behind us
3. From **above** – by reflecting on revelation. Since we are incapable of observing certain realities before death - the Day of Judgment, Paradise, Hell, etc. – these can only come from Allah ﷻ.

In this section, Allah ﷻ says for those who disbelieve that He has put a wall in front of them and behind them, and He has put collars on their necks. They look up, yet they have been covered and they cannot see. Guidance has been cut-off for them in all three of the aforementioned directions.

Thus, they are blinded from all sides and therefore cannot see guidance properly. In the following sections we will see how Allah ﷻ expands upon this notion of the avenues for guidance further.

The next section focuses on the second of these avenues for guidance; history. Specifically, we will look at how this passage highlights the disbeliever's refusal to learn from the past.

Lessons From History (The Wall Behind Them) – Ring Structure Of *Āyāt* 13-32

E - Give them an example of the residents of a town, when the messengers came to them. We sent them two messengers, but they rejected both. (13) So, We reinforced [the two] with a third, and they declared, "We have indeed been sent to you [as messengers]." (14)

F - The people replied, "You are only humans like us, and the Most Compassionate has not revealed anything. You are simply lying!" (15) The messengers responded, "Our Lord knows that we have truly been sent to you. (16) And our duty is only to deliver [the message] clearly." (17) The people replied, "We definitely see you as a bad omen for us. If you do not desist, we will certainly stone you [to death] and you will be touched with a painful punishment from us." (18) The messengers said, "Your bad omen lies within yourselves. Are you saying this because you are reminded [of the truth]? In fact, you are a transgressing people." (19)

G - Then from the farthest end of the city a man came, rushing. He advised, "O my people! Follow the messengers. (20) Follow those who ask no reward of you, and are [rightly] guided. (21) And why should I not worship the One Who has originated me, and to Whom you will be returned. (22) How could I take besides Him other gods whose intercession would not be of any benefit to me, nor could they save me if the Most Compassionate intended to harm me? (23) Indeed, I would then be clearly astray. (24) I do believe in your Lord, so listen to me." (25) [But they killed him, then] he was told [by the angels], "Enter Paradise!" He said, "If only my people knew (26) of how my Lord has forgiven me, and made me one of the honorable." (27)

F' - We did not send any soldiers from the heavens against his people after his death, nor did We need to. (28) It was no more than a single Cry, and in no time, they were extinguished. (29)

E' - Oh pity, such beings! No messenger ever came to them without being mocked. (30) Have the deniers not considered how many peoples We destroyed before them who never came back to life again? (31) Yet they will all be brought before Us. (32)

CONNECTIONS

[E]/[E'] - Allah ﷻ begins the section by giving us an example of a town which had messengers sent to it. The corresponding passage addresses those who reject the messengers. It is as if the latter section is rhetorically asking "How many other towns are there? How many more examples do you need?"

[F]/[F'] - Section **[F]** describes the messengers speaking softly and lovingly to their audiences' ears. In response, the disbelievers mocked and cursed them. As a consequence of their misdeeds, they are destroyed by a loud cry that brings death.

[G] - This section beautifully transitions between the outer sections. It describes a man who came from the furthest part of the city (Sections **[E]/[E']**) and delivered a message (Sections **[F]/[F']**).

Lessons from the World Around Us (The Wall in Front of Them) – Mirror Structure of Āyāt 33-44

H - And a miraculous sign for them is the dead earth. We have brought it to life and brought forth from it grain, and from it they eat. (33) And We placed therein gardens of palm trees and grapevines and caused to burst forth therefrom some springs - (34) That they may eat of His fruit. And their hands have not produced it, so will they not be grateful? (35) Exalted is He who created all pairs - from what the earth grows and from themselves and from that which they do not know. (36)

> **I** - And a miraculous sign for them is the night. We remove from it [the light of] day, so they are [left] in darkness. (37)

>> **J** - And the sun runs [on course] toward its stopping point. That is the determination of the Exalted in Might, the Knowing. (38) And the moon - We have determined for it phases, until it returns [appearing] like the old date stalk. (39)

>> **J'** - It is not appropriate for the sun to reach the moon,

> **I'** - nor does the night overtake the day, but each, in an orbit, is swimming. (40)

H' - And a miraculous sign for them is that We carried their children in a laden ship. (41) And We created for them from the likes of it that which they ride. (42) And if We should will, We could drown them; then no one responding to a cry would there be for them, nor would they be saved (43) Except as a mercy from Us and provision for a time. (44)

CONNECTIONS

[H]/[H'] – Of Allah's signs is that He brings the dead earth back to life. The corresponding section describes a situation where mankind was in the middle of the sea, as good as dead, but Allah ﷻ kept them alive, thus granting them another chance at life. Allah ﷻ mentions fruits and provisions, which matches with those embarking on the ship seeking provisions. He ﷻ sends down water from the sky to give life, while those on the boat are reminded that had He wanted, the water could also serve as a source of death. Finally, Allah ﷻ mentions His creation of spouses and of things in pairs. The complementary section speaks of children and offspring — the outcome of spouses being paired together - boarding the ship.

[I]/[I'] – Both sections describe *al-layl (the night)* and *an-nahār (the day)*, and in that order.

[J]/[J'] – Both sections describe *ash-shams (the sun)* and *al-qamar (the moon)*, and in that order.

The Blind (The Covering) – Ring Structure of Āyāt 45-47

<table>
<tr><td>K - But when it is said to them, "Beware of what is before you and what is behind you; perhaps you will be shown mercy... " (45)</td></tr>
<tr><td>L - And no sign comes to them from the signs of their Master except that they are from it turning away. (46)</td></tr>
<tr><td>K' - And when it is said to them, "Spend from that which Allah has provided for you," those who disbelieve say to those who believe, "Should we feed one whom, if Allah had willed, He would have fed? You are not but in clear error." (47)</td></tr>
</table>

CONNECTIONS

[K]/[K'] – Both sections begin with *"wa idhā qīla la-hum (and when it is said to them)."* Both sections converge on highlighting the crimes of the disbelievers. [K] mentions their lack of God-consciousness ("beware") while Section [K'] mentions their lack of care for humanity.

[L] – The disbelievers are heedless of the "signs of their Master", with the Master, Allah ﷻ, representing "what is above." They have resolved to deny all advice and miracles sent to them. They have become willfully blind by "turning away."

Lessons from the Unseen (Guidance from Above) – Ring

Structure of *Āyāt* 48-68

M- And they say, "When is this promise, if you should be truthful?" (48)

> **N** - They will not see anything but a single loud cry which will seize them while they are disputing. (49) And they will not be able [to leave] any will, nor to their people can they return. (50)

>> **O** - And the Horn will be blown; and at once from the graves to their Master they will hasten. (51) They will say, "O [what terrible destruction has fallen upon] us! Who has raised us up from our sleeping place?" [The reply will be], "This is what the Most Merciful had promised, and the messengers told the truth." (52) It will not be but a single loud cry, and at once they are all brought present before Us. (53) So today no soul will be wronged at all, and you will not be recompensed except for what you used to do. (54)

>>> **P** - Indeed, the companions of Paradise, that Day, will be amused in [joyful] occupation - (55) They and their spouses - in shade, reclining on adorned couches. (56) For them therein is fruit, and for them is whatever they request [or wish] (57) [And] "Security," a word from a Merciful Master. (58)

>> **O'**- [Then He will say], "But stand apart today, you criminals. (59) Did I not enjoin upon you, O children of Adam, that you not worship Satan - [for] indeed, he is to you a clear enemy - (60) And that you worship [only] Me? This is a straight path. (61) And he had already led astray from among you much of creation, so did you not use reason? (62) This is the Hellfire which you were promised. (63) [Enter to] burn therein today for what you used to deny." (64) That Day, We will seal over their mouths, and their hands will speak to Us, and their feet will testify about what they used to earn. (65)

> **N'** - And if We willed, We could have obliterated their eyes, and they would race to [find] the path, and how could they see? (66) And if We willed, We could have 2deformed them, [paralyzing them] in their places so they would not be able to proceed, nor could they return. (67)

M' - And whomever We give old age, We reverse him in creation; so will they not understand? (68)

CONNECTIONS

[M]/[M'] – This ring begins with the disbelievers asking, "When is this promise?" They mockingly want to know when they will be resurrected and presented before Allah ﷻ. Their question is later responded to in [M'] when they are told that we are all aging. In other words, "Look at your body deteriorating. As you age, the promise is being fulfilled. You are already slowly being brought back to Allah ﷻ."

[N]/[N'] – Both parts use the same wording of *"wa lā yarjiʿūn (they will not return)"* to describe the desperate situation of the disbelievers on the Day of Judgment. They both also make reference to sight with words such as *"yubṣirūn (they see),"* *"aʿuni-him (their eyes)"* and *"yanẓurūn (they look)."*

[O]/[O'] – Both **[O]** and **[O']** describe scenes from the Day of Judgment. **[O]** ends with Allah ﷻ saying, "you will not be recompensed except for what you used to do," and **[O']** ends with the limbs testifying against their user "about what they used to earn."

[P] - The chaos depicted in the surrounding sections is centered by a pleasant description of the people of Paradise.

Quran and Allah's Decree – Ring Structure of *Āyāt* 69-83[28]

> **Q** - And We did not give Prophet Muhammad, knowledge of poetry, nor is it befitting for him. It is not but a message and a clear Quran (69) To warn whoever is alive and so that the verdict will become deserving on the disbelievers. (70)
>
>> **R** - Did they not see that We have created for them from what Our hands have made, cattle, and [then] they are their owners? (71) And We have tamed them for them, so from it [are the ones] they ride, and from it [are the ones] they eat. (72) And for them therein are benefits and drinks, so will they not be grateful? (73)
>>
>>> **S** - But they have taken besides Allah [false] deities that perhaps they would be helped. (74) They cannot help them, and they [themselves] are going to be soldiers present against them. (75)
>>>
>>>> **T** - So do not let their speech grieve you. Indeed, We know what they hide and what they declare. (76)

---

28   Khan's work on this section is also built off of the observations made by Neal Robinson in <u>Discovering the Qur'an</u> (London: SCM Press Ltd, 1996), pages 151-152

> **S'** - Has the human being not observed that We created him from a [mere] sperm-drop - then all of a sudden, he makes clear arguments [against Allah]? (77) And he presents for Us an example [i.e., false philosophies against Us] and forgets his [own] creation. He says, "Who will bring bones back to life while they are decaying?" (78)
>
> **R'** - Say, "The one who brought them to life the first time will give them life [again]; and He is Knowledgeable over all [manner of] creation." (79) [It is] He who made for you from the green tree, fire, and then from it you ignite. (80) Is not He who created the skies and the earth Able to create the likes of them? Of course, [it is so]; and He is the Ultimate Creator, Entirely Knowledgeable. (81)
>
> **Q'** - His command/decision is only when He intends a thing that He says to it, "Be," and it is. (82) How perfect is the one in whose hand belongs the kingdom of all things, and to Him alone you will be returned. (83)

CONNECTIONS

[Q]/[Q'] - The section begins with describing the words of Allah ﷻ (i.e., the Quran) and ends with mention of Allah's word (i.e., His decree). The Quran is the primary method that we learn of Allah's decree.

[R]/[R'] - Here Allah ﷻ mentions His favors and creation. In particular, He highlights the provision He provides mankind in the form of livestock. In the corresponding section, Allah ﷻ again speaks of His ability to create and again mentions provision, but this time He focuses the discussion on the natural resources He provides for mankind in the form of wood and fuel.

[S]/[S'] - This section begins with the tragedy of human beings taking gods besides Allah ﷻ, even though those false gods cannot aid them. This is paralleled by the tragedy of human beings forgetting their own creation. At this point the disbeliever has shed all humility and incredulously says, "Who will bring bones back to life while we are decaying?"

[T] - The entire passage centers on the words of others - "Do not worry about what they say" - which ties back to the opening and closing in **[Q]/[Q']**.

Organization of the Entire Sūrah

Now that we have observed the coherence of the six individual passages, we can bring them altogether to show their coherence as a *sūrah* as well.

When viewed in totality, the passages form what appears to be a larger ring structure.

<table>
<tr><td>U - Quran and Our Record (1-12)</td></tr>
<tr><td>V - History — The Wall Behind Us (13-32)</td></tr>
<tr><td>W - World Around Us — The Wall in Front of Us (33-44)
W' - Blind — The Covering (45-47)</td></tr>
<tr><td>V' - Judgment in Afterlife - Guidance from Above (48-68)</td></tr>
<tr><td>U' - Quran and Allah's Decree (69-83)</td></tr>
</table>

CONNECTIONS

[U]/[U'] – The sūrah opens and closes with the document (Quran) and command of Allah ﷻ (His decree).

[V]/[V'] – Learning from our past is coupled with judgment in the future.

[W]/[W'] – Observing the world around us is coupled with blindness and the inability to do so.

One Big Ring Structure

It has been proposed that *Sūrat YāSīn* can also be organized into one large ring structure when one considers the *āyāt* on an almost individual level. [29]

<table>
<tr><td>A — What Allah ﷻ sent (1-4)</td></tr>
<tr><td>B — Allah's word (5-7)</td></tr>
<tr><td>C — Hell (8-10)</td></tr>
<tr><td>D — Implicit reference to Paradise (11)</td></tr>
<tr><td>E — The Revival and our record (12)</td></tr>
<tr><td>F — Examples for them (13-14)</td></tr>
<tr><td>G — "Human beings like us" (15-17)</td></tr>
</table>

---

29   These observations owe to the work initiated by:

Symmetry in Sura al-Yasin. The Gold Mine Initiative. (2018, June 9). Retrieved 2022, from https://tgminitiative.blogspot.com/2018/06/symmetry-in-sura-al-yasin.html

Though his original structure left out some *āyāt*, I was able to build off his proposed ring structure to arrive at my own organization that included every *āyah*. I'll be the first to admit that I'm not that too convinced that this ring works, but I want to document it so that someone more capable can build upon it in the future. And, yes, he called it "Sura al-Yasin" with an extra "al-" in there, which is probably a small oversight since most suwar start with "al-."

H – Disbelievers verbally abusing messengers and the messengers responding (18-19)

I – Worship the Creator or face the consequences (20-29)

J – Alas for My servants! How many generations have We destroyed before them? (30-31)

K – All will be presented before Allah ﷻ for judgment (32)

L – Worldly gardens, fruits, and pairs (33-36)

M – Night and Day (37-40)

N – Offspring carried on the boat (41-42)

O – Could drown without a response to their cry (43-44)

P – Said to them... (45)

Q – No sign except they turn away (46)

P' – Said to them... (47)

O' – Single cry takes them away (48-49)

N' – No bequest and no going back to family (50)

M' – Resurrection and accounting (51-54)

L' – Paradise, fruits, and pairs (55-58)

K' – Guilty will be separated out for judgment (59)

J' – Didn't I warn you? Satan led astray many generations before you (60-62)

I' – Worship the Creator or face the consequences (63-75)

H' – Don't let what they say grieve you (76)

G' – Creation of human beings (77)

F' – Example for Us (78a)

E' – Who will revive decayed bones? He knows all (78b-79)

D' – Green trees (80a)

C' – Fire (80b)

B' – "Be" and it is (81-82)

A' – We will return to Allah ﷻ (83)

CONNECTIONS

[A]/[A'] – The *sūrah* begins with Allah ﷻ swearing an oath by the Quran. This oath is to emphasize what He has sent, i.e., the Messenger ﷺ. The ending emphasizes our **return** to Him.

[B]/[B'] – The Revelation (Allah's Word) is spoken of next, along with the fact that the *"qawl (word)"* (i.e., judgment) has been established upon most, but they still refuse to believe. The corresponding section gives us a taste of the power of Allah's speech. All He needs to do is *"yaqūl (say),* "Be," and it is.

[C]/[C'] – Allah ﷻ describes the state of the Hell-bound people on the Day of Judgment as having chains around their necks and there being barriers propped up in front of and behind them. The paired section mentions *"fuel"* for fire, which might be a subtle reference to another attribute of those condemned to Hell.[30]

[D]/[D'] – There is an implicit reference to Paradise wherein Allah ﷻ says to give good news of "forgiveness and a generous reward." The complementary section gives another implicit reference to gardens with the mention of "green trees."

[E]/[E'] – Allah ﷻ informs us that He is the One who will *"nuḥyī (revive)"* the dead and that He records every detail about our lives. Similarly, the end has the disbelievers asking, "Who will *'yuḥyī (revive)'* decayed bones?" Allah ﷻ immediately responds, "He will *'yuḥyī (revive)'* them who produced them the first time." He continues, again referencing His knowledge of all things, "and He is, of all creation, Knowing."

[F]/[F'] – Allah ﷻ introduces the story of the town saying, *"waḍrib la-hum mathalan (Present the example for them)* of the people of the town, when the messengers came to them." Similarly, in the corresponding section He says, *"wa ḍaraba la-nā mathalan (And he presented an example for Us),* while forgetting his own creation." At first it is Allah ﷻ presenting the example to mankind, but the latter half shows the disbeliever arrogantly trying to present an example back to Allah ﷻ.

[G]/[G'] – The disbelievers' initial rejection of the messengers was that they were just "humans beings like us." Allah ﷻ turns this rejection on its head in the complementary section wherein He says, "Does man not consider that We created him from a [mere] sperm-drop - then suddenly he is argumentative?" They want to argue using "human origins" as a proof against the

---

30   See 2:24, "...fear the Fire, whose fuel is men and stones, prepared for the disbelievers."

messengers, and Allah 🕮 replies that it is their very humanity that should prevent them from making such arguments.

[H]/[H'] – The disbelievers of the town begin to verbally abuse their messengers, but the messengers respond back to their provocateurs. The linked section tells the Messenger 🕮 to not grieve their words. He is similarly being mocked by his people, but in this instance, Allah 🕮 goes on the attack for the Messenger 🕮. He 🕮 does not need to defend himself.

[I]/[I'][31] – Following the Messengers' rejection, a believing man came from the end of town to reinforce their message. He says, *"A'attakhidhu min dūni-hi ālihata (Should I take other than Him as a [false] god)?* If the Most Merciful intends for me some adversity, their intercession will not avail me at all, nor can they save me." Similarly, Allah 🕮 says towards the end of the sūrah, *"wattakhadhū min dūn illāhi ālihata (But they have taken besides Allah [false] gods)* so that perhaps they would be helped. But they are not able to help them."

The man further says, "I have believed in my Master, so listen!" The complementary section speaks of Allah's creation of cattle and livestock, and how He made them subservient to us. The connection may not be immediately obvious, but consider that cattle are used in the Quran to describe people who do not listen, and only follow blindly. [32]

After the man is rejected, Allah 🕮 alludes to his death saying that he was entered into Paradise. In the corresponding section, Allah 🕮 speaks of the disbelievers' destiny, saying that they will be entered into Hell because of their disbelief. Their limbs will testify against them (presumably with regards to the killing they did).

In this life, in retaliation for their crime of murder, Allah 🕮 did not send a *"jund (army),"* but instead took them out with a single Shout. The irony being that they used to worship idols which they themselves had to act as the *"jund (army)"* for, since the idols could not speak or defend themselves.

[J]/[J'] – Allah 🕮 laments the state of those who reject faith, asking them

---

31   These sections gave me the hardest time. The observant reader will notice that these sections are the longest in the entire ring. The many connections within there just did not suit a ring structure, so I bunched them all together. Yeah, kind of cheating, I know, but that is the nature of developing research. *In shā' Allah* I will lay the groundwork for someone in the future to build off of to create a much better ring structure.

32   See 25:44 – "Or do you think that most of them hear or reason? They are just like livestock. Rather, they are [even] more astray in [their] way."

to reflect on all the previous generations that He destroyed in the past for their similar transgressions. Later, Allah ﷻ reiterates this point, saying that they should have worshiped Him. Satan has led astray many generations before them.

[K]/[K'] – We are told that all sinners will be brought before Allah ﷻ on the Day of Judgment for their full accounting. Allah ﷻ provides further details later on when He tells us how the criminals will be commanded to stand apart as a form of humiliation before their judgment comes.

[L]/[L'] – Amongst Allah's miraculous signs are the fruits we eat and *"al-azwāj (the spouses and pairs)"* He created. In the linked section Allah ﷻ describes believers in Paradise eating any fruits they wish, reclining with *"azwāju-hum (their spouses)"* in bliss. Those who heed the signs in this life will enjoy them in the next life.

[M]/[M'] – Another miraculous sign from Allah ﷻ is the night and day. Darkness "suddenly" outstrips the day, the sun quickly moves to "a resting place," and the moon goes through phases to help us distinguish the passing of time. Similarly, Allah ﷻ describes the Horn being blow and people "suddenly" rushing out of their graves towards Allah ﷻ. They will say, "Who brought us out of our resting place?" The Horn is then further described as a single cry, which results in everyone being in front of Allah ﷻ without a moment's notice. No time loss in-between steps of the Afterlife.

[N]/[N'] – Allah ﷻ then describes Him carrying our offspring on ships as another miraculous sign from Him. In the same vein, Allah ﷻ says that on Judgment Day, no one will to leave behind a final will [for their family], nor will they be able to return to their families unlike those who leave on ships.

[O]/[O'] – If Allah ﷻ wanted, He could drown those on the ship and no one would respond to their cries, but He typically does not do that through His mercy and respite. On the same note, the Trumpet will blow and take away the argumentative disbelievers with a single cry, and no one will be able to help them then.

[P]/[P'] – Both sections begin, *"wa idhā qīla la-hum (and when it is said to them)..."* First, they are told to be conscious of their actions and what deeds they are putting forth for the Afterlife. In the second instance, they are being scolded, because when they are asked to spend on the poor, they refuse to spend in this life and mock Allah ﷻ, which will lead to consequences in the Next life.

[Q] – At the center of this *sūrah* appears to be a summary of all the outlying parts. "And no sign comes to them from the signs of their Lord except that they are turning away from it." Over and over again, Allah ﷻ gives examples and signs to help guide people to His worship, but they continuously reject faith and go as far as to mock it as well.

Linear Structure of the Sūrah

Between the mention of "Quran" at the beginning and the end of this *sūrah*, it appears we have a chronological timeline of events which gives the *sūrah* a linear structure as well.

Quran → Past → Present → Future → Quran

And Allah ﷻ knows best.

BIBLIOGRAPHY

al-Ālūsī, Maḥmūd ibn ʿAbd Allah. *Rūh al-Maʿānī fī Tafsīr al-Quran al-ʿAẓīm wa al-Sabʿ al-Mathānī*. Beirut: Mu'assasah al-Risālah, 2010

al-Baghawī, al-Ḥussain ibn Masʿūd. *Maʿālim al-Tanzīl*. Saudi Arabia: Dār al-Ṭayyibah, 2010

al-Gharnāṭī, Muḥammad ibn Yūsuf. *al-Baḥr al-Muḥīṭ fī al-Tafsīr*. Makkah: al-Maktabah al-Tijāriyyah

al-Maẓharī, Muḥammad Thanā Allah. *al-Tafsīr al-Maẓharī*. Beirut: Dār al-Kutub al-ʿIlmiyyah, 2007

al-Qurṭubī, Muḥammad ibn Aḥmad. *al-Jāmiʿ lī Aḥkām al-Quran*. Damascus: Mu'assasah al-Risālah, 2013

al-Rāzī, Fakhr al-Dīn. *Mafātīḥ al-Ghayb*. Cairo: Dār al-Ḥadīth, 2012

al-Shawkānī, Muḥammad ibn ʿAlī. *Fatḥ al-Qadīr*. Beirut: Dār ibn Ḥazm, 2005

al-Ṭabarī, Muḥammad ibn Jarīr. *Jāmiʿ al-Bayān ʿan Ta'wīl Āyy al-Quran*. Beirut: Dār ibn Ḥazm, 2013

al-Zūḥailī, Wahbah. *al-Tafsīr al-Munīr fī al-ʿAqīdah wa al-Sharīʿah wa al-Manhaj*. Damascus: Dār al-Fikr, 2009

ibn ʿĀshūr, Muḥammad al-Ṭāhir. *Tafsīr al-Taḥrīr wa al-Tanwīr*. Beirut:

Mu'assasah al-Tārīkh

Ibn Kathīr, Ismā'īl. *Tafsīr al-Quran al-'Aẓīm*. Saudi Arabia: Dār 'Ālam al-Kutub, 2004

Quṭb, Syed. *fī Ẓilāl al-Quran*. Cairo: Dār al-Shurūq, 2009

Shafi, Muhammad. *Ma'riful Qur'an*. Pakistan: Maktaba-e-Darul-Uloom, 2003

ABOUT THE AUTHOR

Shaykh Furhan Zubairi was born in 1983 in Indianapolis, IN. Shortly thereafter, he moved and spent most of his youth in Southern California, graduating from high school in Irvine in 2001. He began his pursuit of Islamic knowledge and spirituality at the Institute of Knowledge (IOK) in 1998 where he started the memorization of the Quran and studied the primary books in the Islamic sciences and Arabic language. After starting college, he took a break and went to Karachi, Pakistan for 9 months to complete the memorization of the Quran at Jamiʿah Binoria. He returned home and completed his B.S. in Biological Sciences from the University of California, Irvine in 2005. He then traveled to Egypt to further his studies of the Arabic language. Thereafter, his pursuit of Islamic knowledge led him back to Pakistan where he completed a formal ʿAlamiyyah degree (Masters in Arabic and Islamic Studies) at the famous Jamiʿah Darul-Uloom in Karachi, where he studied with prominent scholars. He has obtained numerous ijaazaat (traditional licenses) in the six authentic books of hadith Siha Sittah as well as the Muwattas of Imam Malik and Imam Muhammad and has also received certification in the field of Islamic Finance. Shaykh Furhan Zubairi serves as the Dean of the Seminary Program (IOKseminary.com) at the Institute of Knowledge in Diamond Bar, CA. He regularly delivers khutbahs and lectures at various Islamic Centers and events in Southern California.